T0010821

One-Minute
PRAYERS®

for

BUSY
PEOPLE

CLAYTON KING

HARVEST HOUSE PUBLISHERS
EUGENE, OREGON

Scripture permissions can be found on page 169.

Cover design by Bryce Williamson
Cover photo © maodesign / Getty Images
Interior design by KUHN Design Group

For bulk, special sales, or ministry purchases, please call 1-800-547-8979.
Email: Customerservice@hhpbooks.com

M This logo is a federally registered trademark of the Hawkins Children's LLC. Harvest House Publishers, Inc., is the exclusive licensee of this trademark.

ONE-MINUTE PRAYERS is a registered trademark of The Hawkins Children's LLC. Harvest House Publishers, Inc., is the exclusive licensee of the federally registered trademark ONE-MINUTE PRAYERS.

One-Minute Prayers® for Busy People

Contents

GOALS

Motivation Matters

Nothing makes me feel better than finishing a hard day's work. Ironically, nothing makes me feel as spent and exhausted as…a hard day's work. So if working hard both fulfills me and wears me out, what's the difference between the kind of work that energizes and the kind that depletes? The answer is in one simple word: motivation. What is the intention behind your hard work? If it's just to gain more (pleasure, possessions, money), then it will deplete you. Proverbs 21:17 says, "Whoever loves pleasure will become poor; and whoever loves wine and olive oil will never be rich." Your motivation matters. Don't kill yourself chasing more, because you'll actually be more miserable than you were in the first place.

God, help me see what motivates my work, and help me work for your glory and not my own gain.

No More Pretending

N one of us would think of ourselves as "wicked," but most of us have projected a version of ourselves to others, online or in real life, that is not accurate to who we really are. It's so easy to paint a picture of ourselves that looks successful, confident, and attractive, but if we're pretending to be these things, we need to think again. Proverbs 21:29 (ESV) says, "A wicked man puts on a bold face, but the upright gives thought to his ways." It's sinful to pretend to be something you're not, but it's honorable to actually think about who you want to be, then pursue the kind of character it takes to become an upright person. Don't get so busy that you don't have time to "give thought to your ways" by asking who you are, what you value, and who you want to become.

Lord Jesus, I want to be an earnest, honest person who doesn't put up a front but reflects who you are to those that you allow me to know and love and influence.

A Good Name

My dad died a decade ago. He was the best man I ever knew. He was a small-business owner in a small southern town, and I worked for him. I watched him treat people fairly, go the extra mile, help people in need, and be generous to his employees. When I go back to my hometown and run into people who knew my dad, they all tell me how much they respected him. Many of them share stories of specific ways my dad helped them when they needed it. My dad still has a good name, even after he's gone. Proverbs 22:1 says, "A good name is more desirable than great riches; to be esteemed is better than silver or gold." Live your life in such a way that your name will outlive your pulse.

God, I need your help to make a name for you instead of working to make sure the world knows my name. May people see your goodness in my life.

New Habits

So many of our habits and personality traits as adults were formed and shaped during childhood. As Proverbs 22:6 says, "Start children off on the way they should go, and even when they are old they will not turn from it." This truth encourages parents to keep loving and caring for and disciplining their children. And it offers all of us understanding and even conviction when we see areas of our lives that we know we need to work on. Good and bad habits are hard to break because many of them were embedded in us at a young age, but by the grace of God (and hard work), when you recognize something that needs to change, you can ask God to help you, and he will. It's never too late to change.

Lord, I confess that I have some bad habits that I need to change. I admit my total dependence on you to help me make the right adjustments and form some new, godly habits in my life.

Resilience

Proverbs 24:16 says, "For though the righteous fall seven times, they rise again, but the wicked stumble when calamity strikes." Tenacity, or endurance, is one quality that you should strive for as a follower of Christ, but how would you gain this potent trait? You have to do more than just read about stamina or study grit in other people. To acquire this valuable characteristic, you have to suffer some setbacks, and no one really enjoys that. You can benefit greatly by learning from your mistakes, by overcoming adversity, by getting knocked down over and over again and continuing to get back up every single time. Don't stay down. Instead of letting the setbacks and suffering make you bitter, let them make you better, stronger, and more resilient for the days ahead.

Prepare me, God, for the hard times that lie ahead of me, and give me a spiritual resilience so that I can bounce back better than I was before.

Minding Your Business

A little sleep, a little slumber, a little folding of the hands to rest—and poverty will come on you like a thief and scarcity like an armed man." The wisdom of Proverbs 24:33-34 is striking! It's an observation of what happens when we procrastinate, when we put off doing the hard work we know we must do and replace it with laziness. There is a time and place for Sabbath, rest, vacation, even an extended sabbatical, but it's essential that we take care of the important business of our lives in order to avoid ruin. What are the essential responsibilities that you need to attend to in your life? Don't neglect your health, your family, your finances, or your relationship with God. Invest time and energy in these areas first, and rest will come more easily.

Holy Spirit, reveal to me any area of importance in my life that I've been blind to. Help me not ignore your voice when you convict me of what I need to change.

Destiny and Eternity

It's so important that we don't let success go to our heads, because when we get cocky, that's often when we become vulnerable to pride. Arrogance is thinking you're better than you really are, an attitude all of us struggle with to some degree. Let the Holy Spirit remind you of this warning in Proverbs 27:1—"Do not boast about tomorrow, for you do not know what a day may bring." You don't have a crystal ball, and you can't tell the future, so it's more helpful to remain humble before God when you make plans. Remember that anything can happen and that no matter what may come, God is ultimately in control of your destiny and your eternity.

Thank you, God, that I have peace knowing that you see the future, you care for me, and you manage the details I could never see or control.

Handcrafted by the Master

N o one knows you better than God. He created you. He formed you. He made you in his image. Take a moment and imagine how much different your life can be when you fully trust him with everything: your thoughts, your fears, your ambitions, your regrets. You don't have to hide anything from God, because he already knows everything about you. Psalm 139:13-14 proves this: "You created my inmost being; you knit me together in my mother's womb. I praise you because I am fearfully and wonderfully made." You were not mass-produced. You were handcrafted by the Master Craftsman.

Help me see myself as you see me, Creator
God. I bear your image, and I am honored
that you would make me in your likeness.

Daily Self-Denial

As you go about your busy day, find some inspiration from the prayer that King David prayed as he made an oath to God that he would place the Lord first in his life. Psalm 132:1-5 says, "LORD, remember David and all his self-denial. He swore an oath to the LORD, he made a vow to the Mighty One of Jacob: 'I will not enter my house or go to my bed, I will allow no sleep to my eyes, or slumber to my eyelids, till I find a place for the LORD, a dwelling for the Mighty One of Jacob.'" How would your life change if you approached your relationship with God like this, with this kind of passion and resolve?

God, I want to want you. Give me a deeper desire for intimacy with you on a daily basis, where all day long I am aware of your presence.

The Ultimate Reward

When living for Jesus is hard, when others ridicule your faith or misunderstand your convictions, one thing to remember is that Jesus promised to reward us in heaven for our faithfulness to him on earth. In Matthew 5:12 Jesus told us to rejoice in hardships because we will be rewarded. Actually, he uses the phrase "great is your reward." Can you imagine how wonderful something is when Jesus calls it "great"? Our ultimate reward for following Jesus is that one day we will actually get to be with him. But isn't it amazing that we get to dream about "great rewards" while we're going through hard times down here on earth?

Help me fix my eyes on eternity today, Jesus,
and not the momentary difficulties I face here
on earth, no matter how hard they may be.

The Company You Keep

One of the most painful trials in life is experiencing disappointment caused by a friend. Nothing hurts as bad as being betrayed or let down by someone you trusted. Proverbs 18:24 says, "One who has unreliable friends soon comes to ruin." Eventually, the company you keep will affect you in a positive or negative way, and negative friends will affect you…negatively. But the second part of that verse says there is a friend who sticks closer than a brother. That's the kind of person you can count on, and that's the kind of friend we all need. The good news is, you can decide who your friends are. So I encourage you today to be friends with trustworthy people who have character and integrity. You'll be glad you did.

Guide me, Holy Spirit, as I meet new people and forge new friendships, and help me to continue investing in the healthy friendships I already have.

Drop It and Defuse It

My dad used to say that the best way to end an argument is to avoid it in the first place. He was spot-on! Proverbs 17:14 says, "Starting a quarrel is like breaching a dam; so drop the matter before a dispute breaks out." When it comes to living at peace with your friends, your family, or your coworkers, you have the power to defuse the ticking time bomb. You don't have to attend every fight you're invited to. You don't have to voice your opinion on every single Facebook post you read. And you don't have to always speak your mind. It is totally within your power to keep your mouth closed and your mind open. Don't break the dam that's holding back the floodwaters. Listen more than you speak, and you can avoid a majority of the drama in your life.

Heavenly Father, you've given me ears to hear your voice, so I will tune them to listen when you speak as you protect me from destruction and regret.

Serving in Secret

When I was in high school, I was at a big church event, and I wanted the pastor to notice me. Hoping he'd invite me to preach at this event in the future, I found him, introduced myself, and began telling him all the places I'd preached and how many people I'd seen come to Christ as a teenager. He gently said, "That's so great to hear, Clayton. I'm really proud of you. Tell me, where do you serve God where no one can see you?" Wow! I was immediately convicted. In Matthew 6:1 Jesus said, "Be careful not to practice your righteousness in front of others to be seen by them. If you do, you will have no reward from your Father in heaven." God sees us serving him even when no one else does.

Holy Spirit, reveal the places where I can serve you without being seen. Reveal the people I can serve with no expectation of return.

The Destructive Power of Pride

Proverbs 16:18 says, "Pride goes before destruction, a haughty spirit before a fall." When we place ourselves at the center of our world, everything can go spinning out of control. The real power to fight pride and be humble isn't found within us at all—it's Jesus. The real power lies with the one who killed pride through his sinless life, sacrifice on the cross, and resurrection from the dead. So take a step back and ponder for a moment: In what area of your life can you cultivate a keener awareness of pride? What will your response be when the Holy Spirit shows you areas of arrogance? Don't argue with God. He loves you. Ask for his help in the places you see pride.

Lord God, I lay my pride before you right now, and I gladly receive your pardon for my sin and my selfishness. I humble myself in your presence and declare that you are my everything.

The Benefit of Discipline

When my son Jacob was little, he would see a car and take off running toward it. Over and over again, Sharie and I would have to grab him to stop the impending accident that awaited him on the asphalt. He would beg us to let him go, but we saw the outcome when he could not. Because we loved him, we stopped him before he hurt himself. On a much larger scale, God will not sit by while his children destroy themselves. He's willing to discipline us, and his discipline is often painful in the moment. When you understand how this process works, you're on the path to wisdom. You can embrace a holy reverence for God and a fear of what would happen to you if you failed to surrender control to him.

Lord, today I will remember Proverbs 1:33—
"But whoever listens to me will live in safety
and be at ease, without fear of harm."

The Wisdom of Humility

P roverbs 11:2 (CSB) says, "When arrogance comes, disgrace follows, but with humility comes wisdom." There's nothing sinful about being proud of a job well done or a goal accomplished. Sinful pride, however, grows from a place of self-sufficiency that assumes we can do it all without God. When we are so consumed with ourselves that we can't see our ultimate need for God, or the needs of others, that's an indication that an attitude of arrogance is leading us to self-dependency. Remember, your attitude always precedes your actions, and arrogance always precedes disgrace. But a life of dependence on God properly aligns our abilities and desires in submission to his sovereignty and grace.

I want my life and my desires to be aligned with your heart, heavenly Father. I know that I lack humility at times, so I rely on you to supply what I need.

A Firm Foundation

Proverbs 10:25 paints a vivid picture of the difference between the way a godly person endures adversity and the way a wicked person is affected by hard times: "When the storm has swept by, the wicked are gone, but the righteous stand firm forever." Regardless of whether a person is a Christian or not, each of us will experience hard times, loss, and difficulty. The difference is stark, however, in how we respond to these issues and trials. When your life is built on the foundation of Christ, you can withstand the storms. If not, you are swept away by them. The Christian life is marked by resiliency.

God, make me a resilient Christian who isn't swayed by the blowing winds of the times I live in. My foundation is secure because my life is built on your promises and your faithfulness.

PRAYER

Pray First, Plan Second

I spend a great deal of time every single week making plans. Because I'm the president of a nonprofit ministry and a pastor at a church, a big part of my job and calling is to plan things out: hiring staff, creating events, writing sermons and books (like this one). But I've learned the hard way that even though I can fill hours of my day making plans about the future, ultimately my hard work in *planning* the future is not what creates the future. Proverbs 21:30 makes that clear: "There is no wisdom, no insight, no plan that can succeed against the LORD." So before you go off with your grand plans for what's to come, have you prayed about them? Have you asked God for his wisdom to carry out his divine blueprint? Remember, his plans always work, and they never fail.

Almighty God, show me what you want for me, and whatever assignment you place before me I will work with all my might to complete.

Pray for Wisdom

When I wake up in the morning, one of the first things I do is make a list of everything that needs to be done that day: meetings, emails, appointments, phone calls. I find myself praying throughout the day for God to help me get it all done, for the energy and focus to finish the list. But what if I prayed for wisdom the same way I prayed for focus and energy? Proverbs 24:14 promises, "Know also that wisdom is like honey for you: if you find it, there is a future hope for you, and your hope will not be cut off." We need to ask God for wisdom as much as we ask for anything else—not only is it extremely valuable and necessary for a life that glorifies God, but it's also the best investment for a future filled with hope, happiness, and joy.

As I trust you for focus and energy every day, Lord,
may I also seek your wisdom and discernment
to guide me as I work, love others, and make
decisions that affect my life and the lives of others.

Illumination

I've been a Christian for thirty-five years, and I confess there are things I read in the Bible that I still don't always understand. I used to get frustrated at my lack of insight, but now I try to practice a simple spiritual discipline that has helped me move out of frustration mode when I feel like I'm in the dark. I stop and I pray, and I ask the Lord to help me understand what's right in front of me. This is a practice the people of God have been doing for thousands of years. Psalm 119:18 says, "Open my eyes that I may see wonderful things in your law." What a beautiful prayer to pray! God alone has the power to give you fresh insight into the Bible. After all, he wrote it. So don't be shy. Ask him for his help. He won't turn you down.

*God, I will pray the same prayer that your
people have prayed for generations: Open my
eyes that I may see beautiful things in your law.*

Prayer, Praise, and God's Presence

A small but powerful daily habit that can help you begin your day in the presence of God is found in Psalm 141:2, which says, "May my prayer be set before you like incense; may the lifting up of my hands be like the evening sacrifice." It was tradition for the Jewish priests to start their day burning incense in the temple and to end their day before God with a sacrifice. What if you did something similar to this, beginning your day with a short prayer and ending your day in praise to God? Don't you think this would have a profound effect on your attitude and overall perspective?

Today I consecrate myself to you, Oh Lord. Help me develop the daily discipline of starting and ending my day in your presence through prayer and praise.

Run to God, Rest in God

I f you've ever been overcome by fear or anxiety, you know how overwhelming it can be to even breathe. As long as we live in this world, we will have to face fear and deal with it one way or another. But instead of numbing ourselves with drugs or alcohol, or avoiding scary things by distracting ourselves with pleasure or entertainment, we can run to God for courage. Psalm 138:3 is a powerful promise: "When I called, you answered me; you greatly emboldened me." Rest in this knowledge when you feel afraid. Through prayer, God alone can make you bold in the face of fear.

> *Father, I need your courage when I feel*
> *fear. I need your sustaining power when I*
> *can't face the things that overwhelm me. I*
> *believe your promise. Strengthen my heart.*

Pray and Walk Away

Sooner or later, for all of us, there comes a time in our work when it's important to realize we may not be able to get it all done. That's when you have to tell yourself that it's okay to leave the project where it is, that it's okay to take a break and breathe. Your work will still be there tomorrow. Your responsibility is primarily to God and to your family, but also to yourself, to care for your own mind and soul. All work and no play...leads to a stroke! Consider this poignant word from Psalm 127:2—"In vain you rise early and stay up late, toiling for food to eat—for he grants sleep to those he loves." Sometimes the best thing you can do is to simply pray and walk away from your work, and rest.

God, I need to trust you more with my work,
my projects, and my rest. I don't have to get it
all done right now. Give me the grace to rest.

Before Dawn

I f you're serious about growing stronger in your faith and deeper in your relationship with Jesus, the most practical thing you can do is to get up early in the morning and spend the first part of your day in uninterrupted time with him. During the hushed moments that encompass the rising of the sun, you inevitably encounter fewer distractions. Most people are sleeping. It's quiet. Your mind is uncluttered. This has been the single most transformative discipline I've applied to my relationship with Jesus—and it works! Psalm 119:147 says, "I rise before dawn and cry for help; I have put my hope in your word." The combination of God's Word and early morning prayer is a life changer.

Holy Spirit, give me grace to order my
personal life in such a way that I can spend
time with you and your Word in the early
morning hours before my work begins.

Don't Try to Do It All

One way to center your emotions during a busy day is to pause for a moment and thank God for something good he's given you. The hard part is not finding something to be thankful for—all we have to do is look around us to see a countless number of God's blessings. The hard part is actually taking time (or I should say, making time) to just stop. We're living in a culture that often feels like a current: a rushing river of endless tasks, to-do lists, errands, responsibilities, and meetings. Do you ever feel like you'll never get it all done? Of course you do. And that's okay because you don't have to do it all. Take a moment to do just one thing. Stop and breathe—and thank God for being so good to you.

Almighty God, I just want to stop right now and tell you how much I love you! Thank you for how good you have been to me.

Feelings and the Flesh

Over the years, I've learned a small discipline that helps me when I'm feeling unsettled about a situation or bothered by something that someone has said or done. When I don't know if it's the Lord stirring my heart, or just my own insecurities or selfish desires within me, I just stop and pray, "Lord, is this feeling from you? Or is it from my flesh?" Proverbs 17:3 says, "The crucible for silver and the furnace for gold, but the LORD tests the heart." In the same way that heat refines precious metals and rids them of their impurities, the Holy Spirit can show us where our desires and emotions come from. Asking the Lord to reveal the source of your emotions is a great way to find peace and stay connected to God throughout your busy day.

Reveal to me, Holy Spirit, the source of my fears, my frustrations, my doubts, my anxiety, and my worries. I trust you to shine a light into the deepest places of my heart.

The Reward of Prayer

Some people don't mind praying out loud in front of others—that would be me. But others get nervous and would rather keep their prayers to God personal and private. I get it. We all have different personalities and Enneagram numbers (if you're into that). But Jesus told us to make sure that when we pray, we're actually talking to God and not performing for an audience. In Matthew 6:5 he said, "When you pray, do not be like the hypocrites, for they love to pray standing in the synagogues and on the street corners to be seen by others. Truly I tell you, they have already received their reward." They were using prayer as a way to get what they really wanted: the praise of other people. Let's make sure that prayer for us is always about connecting with our Father, and not about any other desire or agenda.

Teach me to pray to you, Lord, in such a way that it comes naturally, like a conversation between two old friends who know and trust each other completely.

Remember the Relationship

The idea of prayer can be confusing and even intimidating for some of us. I mean, who am I that I should speak to God? What do I say to him? ("Good morning?" "How was your day?") And should I pray in a British accent or speak in King James English? Well, let me encourage you: It's actually not that complicated, and you don't have to plan out some elaborate prayer to impress God. In Matthew 6:7-8 Jesus said, "When you pray, do not keep on babbling like pagans, for they think they will be heard because of their many words. Do not be like them, for your Father knows what you need before you ask him." So relax and remember that God just wants a relationship with you. He enjoys spending time with you. It's not so hard when you remember that it's a conversation with your dad.

Heavenly Father, help me uncomplicate my perspective on prayer. Help me remember that I am talking with my Father about the things that I feel and need.

Overlooking Offense

Proverbs 19:11 says, "A person's wisdom yields patience; it is to one's glory to overlook an offense." It takes real humility to ignore an affront, to disregard a put-down, to overlook an insult. For this to be possible, you have to admit you're not too good to forgive someone for hurting your feelings; after all, your feelings are not the end-all in your life. They come and go. Feelings are not to be trusted because they change so rapidly. The smart course of action is to choose to let things go. Don't dwell on the past. Don't rehearse hurtful words. Take the pain to Jesus in prayer. Drop it off at the foot of the cross, and leave the offense with Christ so that you can live free.

*Jesus, because you forgave me of my sins
that offended you, I can learn to forgive
every single person who sins against
me and offends me in any way.*

Repent and Prosper

No one is perfect and everyone sins—including Christians and including you. Until we get to heaven, we'll continue to disobey God at times. The key is to know what to do after you've blown it or messed up again. Our instinct is to sweep our transgressions under the rug and move on to the next thing in our busy lives. But there's a much better way to handle yourself when you sin: Pray and repent. Proverbs 28:13 says, "Whoever conceals their sins does not prosper, but the one who confesses and renounces them finds mercy." Admitting your guilt to God in prayer actually removes the feelings of guilt and gives you access to his mercy and forgiveness.

> *God, I want to experience the sheer joy*
> *of walking through life unencumbered*
> *by the weight of guilt. Help me confess*
> *and repent of sin as soon as I mess up.*

Open Hearts, Open Ears

Proverbs 17:28 says, "Even fools are thought wise if they keep silent, and discerning if they hold their tongues." The meaning here is simple: When you spend all your time talking, you can't hear anything that anyone is saying to you, or even what God may be trying to get you to see and hear. That's what fools do. Maybe it's time to be quiet and stop talking so you can actually hear what God is trying to teach you. Even fools can become wise if they close their mouths and open their ears. But opening your ears begins with opening your heart. Humble yourself and pray, asking God to speak to you, and then be still and quiet and listen to what he says.

My ears and my eyes are wide open for you today, Jesus. Speak to me. Show me more of you. I am waiting and listening.

What You Cannot Do

I t's all too easy to spend your waking hours running around doing an endless number of chores, only to get to the end of the day and wonder what you actually accomplished. Running errands, answering emails, and returning voice mails and text messages can give you a sense of being productive, but small tasks can also distract us from more important eternal work, like prayer, studying the Scriptures, or helping someone in need. Proverbs 21:31 says, "The horse is made ready for the day of battle, but victory rests with the LORD." No matter how much sweat equity you put into a dream or a project or a responsibility, remember that God alone has the final say in the matter. Since victory rests with the Lord, you can rest easy.

*Lord, I believe that you can do what I
cannot do, that you've already won the
ultimate victory over sin and death on my
behalf, so I will rest in your strong arms.*

Stress and Compromise

I've noticed that when successful adults are stressed, they often succumb to the temptation to compromise personal convictions for the sake of having a good time with friends. When you're exhausted, it's easy to "relax" or "blow off some steam" by having a few drinks with your coworkers or even getting in the habit of a glass of wine or a beer before bed to unwind. But be careful. Proverbs 23:20-21 warns about this kind of behavior: "Do not join those who drink too much wine or gorge themselves on meat, for drunkards and gluttons become poor, and drowsiness clothes them in rags." Don't put yourself in a situation where you become dependent on any substance, no matter how harmless it may seem or how many other people may be doing it. Avoid regret by practicing wisdom and self-control.

Jesus, when I'm tired and exhausted, I choose to turn to you for peace instead of to any other source or substance. You are my sustaining joy and power.

Right in Front of You

When you're stressed out with busyness and to-do lists, it's so easy to miss something God may be trying to teach you. One small spiritual discipline that has a big positive impact on your life is learning to stop, just for a moment, and pay attention to what's right in front of you. Being present, noticing your surroundings, paying attention to people and situations—these are the practices God often uses to break through to us, to remind us that he loves us, to nudge us toward an action he wants us to take or a path he wants us to follow. Be encouraged by Proverbs 24:32—"I applied my heart to what I observed and learned a lesson from what I saw." Wisdom and learning are all around you. Be still and quiet long enough to see it and embrace it as a gift of God.

God, I ask for your assistance as I pay attention
to what is right in front of me. Help me focus
on what's happening now instead of trying
to figure out everything that's ahead of me.

Limited Capacity

Be cautious of the desire to always have more: more money, more influence, more opportunities, more projects. God made your heart with limits, and even if you're a high-capacity worker or leader, your capability is not unlimited. There is wisdom in Proverbs 25:16— "If you find honey, eat just enough—too much of it, and you will vomit." The insatiable desire for more can take you to dark places. It can wear you down emotionally and physically. Do you feel the weight of too many responsibilities? Do you have too many plates spinning right now? Do you struggle to sleep at night because you can't turn off your brain? These may be signs that you're overburdened and that you need to off-load something or let something go.

Father, help me acknowledge my limited capacity as a human being. Allow me to find peace in your sovereign ability to take care of all the things that I cannot handle.

The Promise of Protection

Psalm 121:5-8 can bring you great comfort when you don't know how to move forward in a time of uncertainty: "The LORD watches over you—the LORD is your shade at your right hand; the sun will not harm you by day, nor the moon by night. The LORD will keep you from all harm—he will watch over your life; the LORD will watch over your coming and going both now and forevermore." Simply reading this out loud will push away the dark clouds of worry and will dispel the fears of the unknown that lies before you. God is your defender!

Heavenly Father, I cast all my worries and fears down, and I pick up your promise of protection over me. My life and my future belong to you. I rest in the knowledge that I do not have to be afraid of anything.

Wounded by Words

One of the results of living such busy lives is that we often don't realize how our reactions and responses can come across to other people. When our minds are focused on our long lists of things to do, it's so easy to snap at our spouse or be sharp with our kids and never realize that the tone of our words can sting the hearts of those we love. Proverbs 18:14 says, "The human spirit can endure in sickness, but a crushed spirit who can bear?" Ask the Holy Spirit to help you control not only the words you say but also the tone and volume of those words when you say them. Let's strengthen each other's spirits with kind words instead of accidentally crushing them with a harsh response when we're feeling overwhelmed or stressed.

Holy Spirit, I know how it feels to be wounded by words. Stop me from hurting those around me in this way. Instead, empower me to heal others with how I speak to them.

The Cure for Strife

I hear these words a lot these days: *anxiety, stress, worry, triggered.* And they all remind me of a word we see often in the Bible. The word is *strife.* Where does strife come from? And what could you cut out of your life that would reduce anxiety and worry and stress? Decreasing the presence of these noxious spiritual fumes in our lives is actually pretty simple. Just be more careful with what you say and what you talk about. Proverbs 18:6 says, "The lips of fools bring them strife, and their mouths invite a beating." We sometimes spout off our frustrations too quickly or share our opinions too vocally, and the result is increased anxiety and stress. But you can reduce the strife in your life by holding your tongue.

> *Holy Father, today I commit to you*
> *that I do not have to speak out loud*
> *everything that I think in my head. I will*
> *keep my mouth shut when I need to.*

Safety from Stress

My life, since I was a teenager, has been filled with travel. I'm constantly packing a bag, catching a plane, and watching the clock. Stress is a perpetual companion unless I have a release valve that I can turn to lessen some of the anxiety that comes with being on the go so often. I've found that a short, simple pause where I say a quick prayer out loud to God can make all the difference in my attitude. This practice really works. Proverbs 18:10 says, "The name of the LORD is a fortified tower; the righteous run to it and are safe." There is safety and peace to be found in running to God during times of pressure or conflict. Just whispering a short prayer when you're feeling anxious can usher real peace into a challenging and busy day.

I know that you are always with me, Lord. You're right beside me no matter what I face, and I thank you for the comfort your presence brings me.

Laying Down Ambition

Our culture seems to always be chasing more: more money, more success, more opportunities, more influence. But there is a price to be paid for filling our lives with so many things, and we can see it in increasing levels of stress and anxiety. It seems that more people are on medication, seeking professional counseling, or turning to drugs and alcohol to cope with the pressures of life. Proverbs 17:1 says, "Better a dry crust with peace and quiet than a house full of feasting, with strife." Maybe the answer lies in letting go of some ambitions, laying down some of the responsibilities, and enjoying the small things in life. After all, what good is a feast in your own home if you're too burned-out and exhausted to actually enjoy it?

Is there anything in my life, God, that I need to let go of in order to experience more of your peace and your presence daily?

Wage War on Worry

It's normal to worry about things we can't control. I sometimes struggle with stressing over money, my family, the future, and people that I love. But even though we tend to worry like this, as the last several years have proven to all of us, we really can't control anything anyway. Jesus encourages us to wage war on worry. In Matthew 6:25 he says, "I tell you, do not worry about your life, what you will eat or drink; or about your body, what you will wear. Is not life more than food, and the body more than clothes?" The Galileans Jesus was talking to lived on the edge of poverty, so if Jesus tells them they don't have to worry about these things, how much more faith should we have that God will care for us?

*Today I choose to wage war on worry by trusting
in your faithful care and provision for my life,
God. I know you love me and will take care of me.*

WORDS

More Calm, Less Calamity

Have you noticed that when you get too busy, you also simultaneously get more easily aggravated? And when that happens, you also become a little more likely to lose your temper and snap at people? I can't count the number of times I've lost control of my words as a result of just feeling overwhelmed, only to have to apologize later for what I said or how I said it. Proverbs 21:23 says, "Those who guard their mouths and their tongues keep themselves from calamity." Are you so busy with life and family and work that you've forgotten to guard what you say to others? Often, the best way to guard your words is to slow down your life, build margin and space into your day for prayer and worship, and spend more time listening than talking. If you take these steps, you'll spend less time digging out of the calamity and more time enjoying the good things in life.

Holy Spirit, set a guard around my mouth and guide my words so that when I speak, I bring calm instead of calamity.

Do Not Succumb to Sarcasm

It's so easy to become cynical and sarcastic in this culture. We see the hypocrisy in politics. We see double standards for the rich and influential. And we get tired of the media pushing narratives and agendas that go against our beliefs or even common decency. But for the health of our souls, it's essential that we don't succumb to mockery, sarcasm, and bitterness. Proverbs 22:10 issues a strong mandate that is quite helpful: "Drive out the mocker, and out goes strife; quarrels and insults are ended." Guard your life by refusing to grant access to any voice that would stir up strife, fighting, and drama. And guard your own life from going down that path, one that leads only to anxiety and bitterness.

Here and now, God, I commit to you that I will run away from situations and scenarios where I'll be tempted to succumb to sarcasm. Instead, I will guard my soul from its destructive effects.

A Heart to Help

I love the simple wisdom of Proverbs 22:11—"One who loves a pure heart and who speaks with grace will have the king for a friend." According to this verse, there's a powerful connection between your heart and your words. When they work in sequence, even kings (that is, leaders with influence) will trust you. When the motivations of your heart are pure and the words that come from your mouth are kind and filled with grace, people of every background will notice you and even trust you. And why is this? Because so few people have the rare combination of a heart that wants to help others and words that want to bless others. By the power of the Holy Spirit, you can be that kind of person.

God, I desire to speak words that reflect your
love, your wisdom, and your presence in my life.

The Strength of Self-Control

When we think of someone who lacks self-control, our understanding of the term is usually connected to poor habits like overeating, drinking too much, or spending too much money on possessions and experiences one cannot afford. But a lack of self-control can also translate into an unwillingness to say no to the invitations and opportunities that others place in front of you. Proverbs 25:28 says, "Like a city whose walls are broken through is a person who lacks self-control." In other words, the willingness to say no is like a protective wall around your life. It affords you the margin to grow as a person, to rest and enjoy life, to take advantage of the good gifts God has given you. If you say yes to everything, you're not really saying yes to anything. Self-control often sounds like the word *no*.

Lord, I know that self-control works only
when I put myself under your control, so I
dedicate myself today to obey your Word, listen
to your voice, and heed your conviction.

Zero Tolerance

Maybe it's the effect of the Simpsons. Maybe it's the cynicism that grows from around-the-clock news feeds. But our culture has grown increasingly derisive and sarcastic, and it's not a good thing. Sarcasm often covers up personal insecurities and hides secret fears. When we treat others with contempt and distrust, it's sometimes a sign of some trauma or pain deeply embedded in our own souls. I encourage you to make a full stop to using sarcasm. It hurts people, and it's not how we want to be treated. Proverbs 26:18-19 lays out the situation perfectly: "Like a maniac shooting flaming arrows of death is one who deceives their neighbor and says, 'I was only joking!'" Don't act like a maniac, and don't shoot flaming arrows of death at other people.

Please, God, make me sensitive to sarcasm and give me no tolerance for it in my own life. I will use my words to build others up.

The Poison of Gossip

You have the power and autonomy to decide what you will and will not listen to. For example, have you ever found yourself feeling really uneasy and uncomfortable as you listened to gossip about another person? I know I have. I want to encourage you to speak up in those situations and let the speaker know that as a follower of Christ, you don't feel right about being part of a conversation about a person who isn't there. Proverbs 26:22 says, "The words of a gossip are like choice morsels; they go down to the inmost parts." So the simple act of listening to gossip negatively affects your own heart and soul and makes you more likely to begin spreading rumors yourself. Cut it off at the source. Don't entertain those conversations. You can walk away, and you'll be better for it.

Holy Spirit, I need courage to walk away
from conversations that include gossip
and negativity. I don't want my soul to be
affected adversely by the poison of gossip.

Stop Waiting to Be Celebrated

Proverbs 27:2 is fairly blunt when it gives us the instruction, "Let someone else praise you, and not your own mouth; an outsider, and not your own lips." Our society rewards people who boast about their own wins and accomplishments. I'm constantly tempted to turn every conversation back to myself, to something I've done or something I'm struggling with. But what if instead of tooting your own horn, you took this verse to heart and consciously chose to notice the accomplishments and victories of others, to verbally encourage those around you for the things they've done? Just imagine how much joy and hope and confidence you could infuse into others if you looked for every opportunity to notice them and celebrate them. What if everyone did this instead of celebrating themselves?

Lord, with your help, I will begin to speak
words of encouragement and celebration
to everyone I get a chance to bless—instead
of waiting on them to celebrate me.

Blessed by Suffering

n Matthew 5:11 Jesus says that when people insult you or persecute you or falsely accuse you of doing evil, you are, of all things…*blessed*? On the surface, this doesn't seem to make sense. How could we find God's blessing when we're being berated? Actually, the key to this kind of special blessing is not that we are persecuted but that we find ourselves suffering *because of Jesus*. We shouldn't feel godly when people treat us poorly if the reason behind the poor treatment is our own negative outlook. I can't act like a jerk and then rejoice when others return the favor. Following Jesus has a cost, but there's no excuse for his disciples to be unkind or mean-spirited to their neighbors.

Help me today to be kind, compassionate,
and caring, Lord, and to extend grace
to those I meet and work with.

Choose Your Words

Proverbs 17:27 says, "The one who has knowledge uses words with restraint." I'm sure you've heard the old nursery rhyme, "Sticks and stones may break my bones, but words will never hurt me." I've often wondered who in the world wrote that! Because they clearly never went through the negative experience of having words used as weapons against them. You know the power that words have to heal you, to hurt you, to lift you up, to tear you down. So no matter how busy you become, no matter how easy it is to forget the effect your words may have on another person, remember how words affect you when someone else speaks to you. This is a practical way to remind yourself to use your words as tools to build other people up by speaking life into them.

Help me choose my words carefully, God. Help me show restraint when I would rather speak my mind in ways that are not helpful to others.

The Blessing of Building Up

Proverbs 18:21 is one of the most stunning verses in all the Bible. Listen to the simplicity of this: "The tongue has the power of life and death, and those who love it will eat its fruit." What does that last part mean? I believe that's an indication that we can discipline ourselves to love speaking life into other people. We can get into the habit of using words to bless others. When we do, our words bear fruit in their lives, but they also bring life and joy to us as well. There's nothing better than speaking encouragement to a friend or family member and watching their eyes light up with joy. The added benefit is that it also fills us up too. We get the extra blessing of being a blessing to a friend.

Father, what a blessing to use my mouth to bring life to the people I love! Thank you for this amazing gift. I will use it for your glory.

The Gift of Encouragement

I try to make it a habit to spend some time every single day encouraging at least one person. Whether my support comes in the form of a text, a phone call, an email, or even a pat on the back and a kind word, I find that my disposition is changed when I take this promise from Proverbs 18:20 literally: "From the fruit of their mouth a person's stomach is filled; with the harvest of their lips they are satisfied." This means that you can decide to use your mouth and the words you speak not only as a means to bless other people but also to encourage yourself! Could you use more encouragement in your life? Sure you could. Simply speak encouraging words to others and watch your own spirit be lifted up in the process.

*Lord, help me find true inward satisfaction
by using my lips to give you praise for who
you are and what you have done in my life.*

Clean Out the Clutter

Proverbs 18:4 is a truly thought-provoking verse: "The words of the mouth are deep waters, but the fountain of wisdom is a rushing stream." Consider the difference—deep waters and a rushing stream. The words we speak are deep waters, meaning that words spoken out loud have the power to go deep down into our hearts where they lodge into our memories. But the wisdom of God's Word is like a powerful river that moves quickly, cleaning out the clutter and removing the debris and confusion that surrounds us. Take some time today to consult with God and ask him for a rushing stream of wisdom to help you along your journey.

*Flush out all the negativity and temptation today,
Jesus, by washing me clean with your perfect
Word and filling me up with your wisdom.*

Watch Your Words

Have you noticed that the busier you become, the easier it is to let your words fly? We lose the filter on our thoughts when we fill our lives with event after event and commitment after commitment. Proverbs 18:7 is a timely warning to be aware of how much trouble we can get into when we forget to tame our tongue: "The mouths of fools are their undoing, and their lips are a snare to their very lives." When we're tired or worn out, it's so easy to say something in the moment that we will regret later. But remember, we don't have to live with that regret. By heeding the wisdom and the warning of the Bible, we can avoid the damage done by reckless, careless words.

God, save me from the consequences of speaking reckless words that I would one day regret. Fill me up with goodness and joy in their place.

Nothing in Return

I've learned that there's a big distinction between encouraging someone and flattering someone. Encouragement is a blessing, one that you should give to others regularly. Flattery, however, is forbidden. And the difference between the two? It all lies in motivation. Encouragement comes from a real desire to bless another person with your words, for their sake. Flattery flows from a desire to get something for yourself, from someone else, by saying kind things from a place of deceit. Proverbs 29:5 warns us of the results of relying on flattery: "Those who flatter their neighbors are spreading nets for their feet." Don't trust flattery, and don't use it to serve your self-centered longings and ambitions.

Holy Spirit, show me my true intentions.
Purify my heart so that when I speak a
good word to someone, I do not need
or expect anything in return.

A New Ethical Impulse

The words we say—and how we say them—mirror what takes place deep within us. So, just as with other heart issues, honoring God with our words first requires that our hearts be transformed by the gospel. When Jesus changes our hearts and we receive him as Lord and King, there is a new ethical impulse within us that drives all of our actions, including our speech toward others. The fact is, in order to be the type of person who speaks truth in love to those around us, we must possess a heart that is motivated out of a genuine love for people. Only through love can our words be acceptable and pleasing to God.

Today, God, I will remember the wisdom of Proverbs 15:23—"A person finds joy in giving an apt reply—and how good is a timely word!"

Words are Powerful

In 1980, my second-grade teacher gave me a nickname: "the mouth of the South." I still remember what she said, verbatim, because she said it to my face—in front of my entire second-grade class. All my friends heard her say it, so of course they called me "mouth of the South" for the rest of second grade. And third grade. And fourth grade. And all the way through to high school. I remember how I felt. James 3:9 says, "With the tongue we praise our Lord and Father, and with it we curse human beings, who have been made in God's likeness." Words are powerful, and part of being a wise follower of Christ is knowing how to use them to give life and not take it. Be intentional and kind with the words you use.

*Fill my heart today with your goodness
and righteousness, heavenly Father, so
that your goodness may overflow
from my mouth when I speak.*

Weapon or Medicine?

Proverbs 12:18 says, "The words of the reckless pierce like swords, but the tongue of the wise brings healing." Careless words thoughtlessly spoken create wounds, but in a beautiful twist, God has given us the gift to heal those wounds with that same medium: words. Using your words to repent and apologize paves the way for healing to begin. Using your words to extend grace finishes the healing work. Words are both good and bad, used for righteousness and evil. They can wound like a weapon, or they can heal like medicine. It's up to us how we use them.

God, I want to be a healer with my words.
Forgive me for the times I've spoken carelessly
and wounded people I love. Use my words
today and in the future as a source of peace and
encouragement for those who need to be lifted up.

Don't Be a Fool

Proverbs 1:7 (CSB) tells us, "Fools despise wisdom and discipline." That's a bold statement. Can you imagine calling someone a fool to their face? Or can you imagine being called a fool, especially by a person you respect or look up to? In our politically correct culture, it's rare to hear such a strong word used to describe someone. So why does the Bible use it? The book of Proverbs uses the word *fool* more than once, actually. The reason God uses such a strong word in Proverbs is for effect. It's really so important to God that he chooses to use a word that is sure to get your attention. He's not being mean. He's being loving and honest.

God, I will not despise your correction in my life. I know it's the proof that I belong to you and that you love me enough to tell me when I am wrong.

The Stress of Indecision

It's better to simply say no than it is to hover around a choice with indecision. When you say yes to something, follow through with it—even if it's hard or inconvenient. If you're not sure about something, then just say no to it, even if it's no for a season. When you straddle the fence on a decision, your lack of commitment doesn't just affect you; it also holds other people hostage. It is inconsiderate of their time, their energy, and their schedules when we go back on our word or renege on an agreement. Don't make excuses. Learn how to look at your schedule and make wise decisions with your yes and your no.

God, empower me today with the simple truth of James 5:12—"All you need to say is a simple 'Yes' or 'No.' Otherwise you will be condemned."

MONEY

The Strength of Storing Up

Much of the stress and worry that burden us stem from a lack of planning. When we fail to plan out our time, our finances, our work, and our investments, that lack of discipline leads to a foreboding sense of impending doom. We wonder what will happen to us if something unexpected occurs. A simple way to fight these fears is to practice the discipline of saving. The book of Proverbs calls it "storing up" and commends it as an alternative to a life of constant worry. Proverbs 21:20 says, "The wise store up choice food and olive oil, but fools gulp theirs down." Don't act like a fool. Say no to what you want now for the sake of peace of mind: a life void of the fear of the future because you prioritized saving, investing, and "storing up."

Lord, show me how to place my trust in your capable hands instead of feeling the pressure to store up enough for my future in my own strength.

Saving over Spending

My father taught me that if I couldn't pay cash for something, I shouldn't buy it. Following this advice would mean that I had to learn how to save money when I made money, which meant that I couldn't spend all the money that I made. It was a hard lesson to learn, but now as a dad and pastor and entrepreneur, I can say it was some of the best wisdom he instilled in me. It turns out this advice comes straight from Proverbs 22:7, which says, "The rich rule over the poor, and the borrower is slave to the lender." I encourage you to do all you can to stay out of debt and to pay off any debts or loans as soon as you can, starting with the smallest and moving toward the biggest. It's liberating to save more than you spend.

Help me, heavenly Father, to know the
difference between what I need and what
I want, and to delay the urge to use debt
to buy what I cannot afford right now.

The Strategy of Generosity

For a Christian, the best investment strategy is generosity. When we give generously, God promises to bless us in ways that don't make mathematical sense. Proverbs 22:9 says, "The generous will themselves be blessed, for they share their food with the poor." So no matter how busy you are with the kids, work, deadlines, laundry, or projects, don't neglect opportunities to share what you have with those in need. God cares for the poor, and he uses us and our resources to provide the things they may not have. Think of it as a great honor...that God would trust you so much that he would ask you to generously share your money, your time, and your attention with his children who need it the most.

Today, Jesus, would you give me a specific opportunity to share my resources with someone that you want me to help and bless because you love them and care for them?

Control or Be Controlled

I t's not a sin to have money, but it's a sin when money has you. We should control where our income goes, but we must fight to not be controlled by the desire for more. That's why Proverbs 23:5 is so stark when it cautions us, "Cast but a glance at riches, and they are gone, for they will surely sprout wings and fly off to the sky like an eagle." As the old phrase says, easy come, easy go. It's foolish to miss the best things in life—family meals, walks with your spouse, gathering with other believers for worship, investing in real friendships—all because you secretly worry about your bank account balance or your retirement fund. Work hard, be generous, and ultimately trust God to provide for you in ways that money never can.

I am fully aware, God, that I cannot control the future, nor can I create a future with my own planning and hard work. I trust you to provide, and I choose to be generous with what I have.

Invest in Eternity

When I was in my midtwenties, I set up a retirement plan. I knew that I needed to plan for the future, and even though retirement was forty or fifty years away, I wanted to get started early. Now that Roth IRA has some value to it. We should all plan for the future, but let's not forget that we will live forever in the new heaven and the new earth. The Bible calls it *eternity*, and Jesus advises us to make sure we plan for it too. In Matthew 6:19-21 he says, "Do not store up for yourselves treasures on earth, where moths and vermin destroy, and where thieves break in and steal. But store up for yourselves treasures in heaven, where moths and vermin do not destroy, and where thieves do not break in and steal. For where your treasure is, there your heart will be." Forever is a long time, and I want my treasure to be waiting for me when I get there.

As I work hard here on earth to be prepared for my future here, help me, Lord, to spend more time preparing for eternity, my forever home with you.

Mastering Your Money

No one likes to think of themselves as a servant to any master. But in reality, we all serve someone or something. Whether it's a boss or a supervisor, a teacher or a coach, or even abiding by the law and paying taxes, we're all serving something. But Jesus warned us to make sure that we never serve the master of money. In Matthew 6:24 he says, "No one can serve two masters. Either you will hate the one and love the other, or you will be devoted to the one and despise the other. You cannot serve both God and money." Jesus knew the kind of power that money can exert on the human soul, so he encourages us to decide that we will serve God first and foremost. When we make that decision, money becomes a tool we can use to live, not a master that we bow down to and serve.

Lord Jesus, you are my Master and King. I give my full allegiance to you, heart and soul, and I commit to not pursuing anything with more passion than I pursue you.

The Way to Walk in Wisdom

Successful, hardworking people face a particular temptation of looking at their achievements and forgetting that all their blessings flow not from themselves, but from the grace and love of God. Proverbs 28:26 says, "Those who trust in themselves are fools, but those who walk in wisdom are kept safe." It's not your retirement account or your life insurance, your income or your checking account balance that will keep you predictably safe in the future. It's a daily desire to know God, to walk in his wisdom, and to make decisions based on what God would have you do instead of what you think will benefit you the most.

Protect me from the foolish notion that I can
secure my future without you, God. I fully
surrender to your sovereign plan for me, knowing
that you will never leave or forsake me.

Deep Roots

Where I grew up, kudzu was everywhere. This plant is tenacious and impossible to kill because of a root system that burrows deep into the soil. If you want to grow, you need roots. If you want to be tough in the face of adversity and steadfast in the face of struggles, take a lesson from the kudzu weed. It's hard to kill and it grows fast on the surface because it has roots extending far under the surface. Proverbs 11:28 (CSB) says, "Anyone trusting in his riches will fall, but the righteous will flourish like foliage." You will wither up and die if you find your identity in your wealth or possessions, but you will flourish (like spiritual kudzu!) if you root your understanding of yourself in God's love for you.

*Lord, I want to have deep roots in Christ
so that I can flourish in this world for your
glory. Show me ways today that I can grow
even deeper in my relationship with you.*

The Vaccine for Greed

Hard work is a blessing that can lead to financial security, but God's financial blessing on your life should also lead to generosity. Proverbs 19:17 promises, "Whoever is kind to the poor lends to the LORD, and he will reward them for what they have done." The vaccine for greed is generosity. Generosity is not about getting money out of your pockets; it's about getting greed out of your heart. We are made in the image of a generous God who gave us his very best and most precious gift: his only Son. We can follow his example, by his Spirit, and choose generosity over greed.

Jesus, all that I have belongs to you, including my finances. Protect me from the sin of greed. I choose generosity instead, and I will look for ways to be kind and willing to share with others.

The Currency of Honor

Proverbs 11:16 says, "A kindhearted woman gains honor, but ruthless men gain only wealth." Do you see that powerful comparison here between these two polar opposites? The woman is honored and respected, but the man is rich. The difference is that she is kindhearted, and he is ruthless. According to the Bible, there's no question which one is best. It's infinitely better to be respected for your integrity than to compromise your character for the sake of financial gain. This is not so much about money as it is about what you choose to value most in your life. Live in such a way that respect is your currency.

God, I would rather be respected than be rich. I prefer living a life of integrity to living a life of luxury. Save me from the trap of chasing wealth by ruthless means.

No Shortcuts

The busier we get, the easier it is to look for shortcuts. We tell ourselves that small compromises will help us catch up or get ahead, but there's always a price to be paid when we take shortcuts, especially with money. It's better to do things the right way so that we don't have to cover our tracks or pay the price later on. Proverbs 12:2 (ESV) says, "A good man obtains favor from the LORD, but a man of evil devices he condemns." What is rewarded in our culture is condemned by God. What good is it to gain an edge or a financial advantage in life if the price you pay is a loss of integrity and the condemnation of the Lord?

God, I don't want to rely on my own craftiness to get ahead or to get caught up. I would rather do things the right way, even if doing so means going slower and getting fewer tasks accomplished.

THE BIBLE

Not Too Busy to Learn

Each of us is given twenty-four hours every single day, and we get to decide how we use that time. It's important that no matter how full your calendar gets, you stay in the habit of learning new information. Researchers have found that stretching your mind with new knowledge keeps the brain fresh and elastic, even warding off cognitive decline. It turns out that the Bible was encouraging people to do this over two thousand years ago. Proverbs 23:12 instructs us, "Apply your heart to instruction and your ears to words of knowledge." So redeem your commute to work by listening to a podcast, a sermon, or a devotional book on Audible. You're never too busy to learn, and you're never so smart that your mind wouldn't benefit from something new and fresh.

Heavenly Father, show me new ways I can redeem the time that I sometimes waste on lesser things, and help me learn new ways of connecting with you.

You Are What You Read

I f you've ever wrestled with impure thoughts, or memories of past sexual sins, or even a wandering eye that sometimes fixates on images that create lustful desires, then you've most likely been frustrated with how quickly those temptations can resurface after you've sworn off them. The key to defeating the powerful pull of wicked desire is to let the Bible be your daily, constant source of strength and guidance. Psalm 119:9 asks a question and then provides the answer: "How can a young person stay on the path of purity? By living according to your word." You cannot live according to God's Word if you don't know God's Word—and you can't know God's Word if you never read the Bible. Make it a daily habit, like brushing your teeth or putting on your seat belt.

God, give me a deep and insatiable hunger to know you by reading your Word, and don't let me go a day without feasting on the Scriptures.

Too Busy Not to Read

There's a direct correlation between how much power sin and temptation have in your life and how much time you spend actually reading the Bible and applying what it says. When your time in Scripture is strong, the influence of the flesh is weakened. For me, I find myself succumbing to anger, impatience, lustful thoughts, and insecurity in seasons when I'm really busy. And guess what also happens in those busy seasons? I usually neglect to spend time in the Bible meditating on Scripture. So when my heart is empty of the power of God's Word, the hunger for sin will fill it, and I find myself giving in. That's what Psalm 119:11 means when it says, "I have hidden your word in my heart that I might not sin against you."

God, I have no excuse whatsoever to neglect the Bible. I am not too busy to eat or breathe, both of which are necessary for life. How much more important to my life is your Word!

Say It Out Loud

Psalm 119:13 is a "cheat code" not only for memorizing Scripture but also for what to do when you find yourself tempted to sin in any number of ways. It says, "With my lips I recount all the laws that come from your mouth." Obviously the writer believed that every word in the Scripture came straight from the mouth of God, and as a result he prioritized speaking the Word of God out loud, with his own lips. There's something quite amazing that happens when we vocalize Scripture, whether from memory or reading straight from the Bible. The more you read the Bible, the more its truth and power will naturally flow from your heart and out of your lips, especially when you're most in need.

Lord, give me the discipline to read and memorize your Word. Give me the courage and boldness to speak Scripture out loud with my own lips.

The Antidote to Anxiety

After all these years, I'm still amazed how practical the Bible is for specific issues that I struggle with. For instance, if you've ever agonized over whether people like you or can't stand you, or if you've ever had people talk about you behind your back, you know how difficult it can be just getting to sleep at night. The constant doubt and questioning really does a number on your insecurities. But Psalm 119:23 gives you the game plan to win that battle. It says, "Though rulers sit together and slander me, your servant will meditate on your decrees." The answer to handling criticism or slander from other people is not to fight fire with fire, but to dig down deep into the Scriptures and simply meditate on God. Just try it. It sounds crazy, but it works.

Father, remind me to run to you and
the timeless truths of your Scriptures
instead of lashing out at others when they
slander me and try to ruin my name.

Turn On the Lights

You make hundreds of small choices every day, and like all of us, you also have to make big decisions that affect you and the people you love. So whether we're assessing what car to buy, what house to purchase, how many children to have, or what job to take, we can always trust that the Word of God will illuminate our decision-making process. Don't try to figure it out on your own, whatever it may be. Go to the Scriptures, and you'll be surprised how much clarity you will receive. Psalm 119:105 promises, "Your word is a lamp for my feet, a light on my path." Turn on the lights by turning to the Bible.

God, when I need to know what I should do,
remind me that I have the greatest resource in
the universe at my fingertips. I will prioritize
the bright light of the Bible in my life.

Make the Effort

Proverbs 18:15 (CSB) says, "The mind of the discerning acquires knowledge, and the ear of the wise seeks it." The way we acquire knowledge is through effort. Our ears seek it out. Our eyes learn to look for it. We glean wisdom from every possible source, beginning with the Bible. We slow down long enough to perceive what God is telling us. We listen more than we talk, we ask questions, we read, we journal, and we learn from mentors. A mark of the presence of Jesus in your heart is that you crave good things more than you crave sin. What are you seeking after? Put forth the effort to grow in the knowledge of the person of Jesus Christ.

Jesus, I really want to know you. I want to experience you as my Savior, my Lord, my Master, and my friend who is always there no matter what I do or what happens.

Don't Just Think It, Say It

The word *encourage* simply means "to give courage" or "to fill with courage." Realize that when you share a verse with a friend, or compliment someone on their appearance or their work, you're actually filling them up with courage to face the day ahead. You're giving them hope to endure their fight against depression, or anorexia, or cutting, or anxiety, or addiction. It's not enough to just think something good and positive about someone. They never benefit from your good thoughts. They only benefit from your encouraging words. It's not your thoughts that give them life—it's the words you share. And what better words can you share than the Bible?

Lord, today I want to live like I really believe Proverbs 10:11—"The mouth of the righteous is a fountain of life." Make me that fountain!

Voices and Choices

Who has your ear? What voices and sources influence your worldview, your beliefs, and your values? Whether you're tuned in to social media or a television network, you're bombarded daily with thousands of subtle and overt messages about what to buy, how you should look, and where you should stand on issues. I encourage you to let the voice of God's Word be the loudest one, the one you listen to most. Ignore the worldly voices that want to pull you from God, that seek to influence you to abandon the Bible and replace it with worldly wisdom. Proverbs 12:5 says, "The plans of the righteous are just, but the advice of the wicked is deceitful." Don't be deceived by sources and voices that you can't trust. Trust God's Word.

Holy Spirit, protect me from the endless noise of the world that tries to tempt me to turn from your paths of righteousness in exchange for empty promises of pleasure.

Building on Bedrock

Proverbs 14:1 gives us a clear comparison between building up and tearing down: "The wise woman builds her house, but with her own hands the foolish one tears hers down." This is the contrast between making wise choices and foolish choices. Like constructing a house brick by brick, board by board, we build our lives with our daily choices. In the same way, consistently making dumb decisions destroys a life slowly but surely. You can look around and see this truth played out in real life. Be like the woman who builds a house with wisdom, and make your life strong by rooting in the solid bedrock of God's Word and wisdom.

Father, I want my life to count. I want my life to last. I want my life to withstand the pressures and powers of this world. I choose to build my life on the firm foundation of your wisdom.

WORK

Working for What You Want

Proverbs 21:25-26 makes a really important comparison between people who refuse to work (they're called sluggards) and people who take pride in the value of work: "The craving of a sluggard will be the death of him, because his hands refuse to work. All day long he craves for more, but the righteous give without sparing." Do you see the stark difference? Lazy people always want what they can't have—and they can't have anything because they don't work. But a righteous person who works hard will have enough stored up that they can share it with others. Make it a goal to use your hard work not just to get what you want but to help others acquire what they need when the occasion arises.

Jesus, Lord of my life, I commit to you
the work of my hands and the resources
that I earn, that it all may be used to
bless others and build your kingdom.

Remember Eternity

Proverbs 22:2 offers a chilling reminder to those of us who rush and hustle and push and grind. It simply says, "Rich and poor have this in common: The LORD is the Maker of them all." Let that be a wake-up call to you, that no matter how much you earn, no matter what accomplishments and achievements and accolades you gain, ultimately you will stand before the One who made you, right alongside outcasts and addicts and alcoholics. Whether you're a president, a prince, or a plumber, God will have the final say in your life, your eternity, and your destiny. Let that motivate you today to do all that you do with God in mind. Work for his glory. Labor for his approval. Do what you do with eternity in mind.

Today, Lord, I confess my total dependence on your power that created me, that saved me, that sustains me, and that will one day carry me into eternity.

Current Behaviors, Future Results

One mark of personal wisdom is the ability to see future results of current behaviors. The wisest people have figured out that certain actions bring specific consequences. For instance, if all you ever do is work, think about work, talk about work, plan work, stress about work, and worry about work, your life will soon become void of any real joy. You'll find it harder to rest and relax, and the people you love the most will probably see it before you do. Take heed of the wise warning of Proverbs 22:3—"The prudent see danger and take refuge, but the simple keep going and pay the penalty." Is there an area of your life where you need to change direction to avoid the impending penalty of your bad habits?

Jesus, I pray you will give me the eyes to see where my decisions are leading me—and the strength to make the changes necessary for a better future.

Make More Margin

Proverbs 22:13 paints a picture of a person who justifies laziness by assuming that the worst-case scenario will happen: "The sluggard says, 'There's a lion outside! I'll be killed in the public square!'" Talk about making up a crazy excuse! How often do we fill our lives to the very margins, wearing ourselves out running from one errand to another, only to realize we still have important duties to attend to, like prayer, exercise, Bible reading, or rest? That's when we typically make excuses. It's so easy to collapse on the couch and binge a Netflix show when there's laundry or dishes to do. Let's not create crazy excuses to justify lazy habits. Instead, let's reorder our priorities and get to work on what's most important.

*Father, I admit that I tend to make excuses.
Remind me that there's no reason for this
because you have given me power and authority
to complete every task that lies before me.*

Added Anxiety Versus Extra Energy

During my childhood, one of my most vivid memories of my father was the steady awareness of how hard he worked, an awareness embodied by a phrase he'd say almost every night. He would announce that he was going to bed, and then he'd give us the reason: "I put in a full day's work, and now I'm worn out. I'm going to sleep good tonight." I always associated hard work with good rest, and this may be a helpful way to distinguish the kind of fatigue that helps you sleep versus the kind that stresses you out. Proverbs 23:4 is a stern warning: "Do not wear yourself out to get rich; do not trust your own cleverness." Are you carrying extra anxiety that saps your energy because you're working just to keep up instead of working to bring glory to God and provide for your family?

Holy Spirit, help me lean on you when I am worn out and remind me that all I do is for the glory of God. I receive your power and will labor with your energy, not my own.

Harmony Is Better Than Balance

t often feels challenging to find the balance between work and rest. Years ago I decided I wasn't going to use the word *balance* anymore. I replaced it with *harmony*. Now I try to harmonize the responsibilities of life and the daily grind, exercise and diet, friendships and family, and I feel less pressure to always strike the perfect "balance." Think of your life more like a symphony and less like a math problem. You're not looking for the perfect balance. You're embracing the rhythms of the season you're in. Proverbs 24:27 says, "Put your outdoor work in order and get your fields ready; after that, build your house." Find the rhythm of work, and order your priorities in harmony with the season of life you're currently in.

Lord, I can only do so much today, and I seek your wisdom in helping me order my priorities according to what is essential and most needed. I leave it all in your hands.

Keep Planting

Don't get discouraged if there's something you've been praying for or working toward for a long time and you haven't seen any fruit yet. Remember Psalm 126:5-6 and the promise found there: "Those who sow with tears will reap with songs of joy. Those who go out weeping, carrying seed to sow, will return with songs of joy, carrying sheaves with them." Now is not the time to quit. Keep sowing seeds in faith. Keep trying and trusting God for a harvest. The abundant yield will come, but you have to keep showing up and doing the work. God operates on a different timetable than you do. And the longer you wait, the sweeter the harvest.

Lord, I admit that there are times I want to give up and throw in the towel, but by your grace I will keep moving forward, trusting you with the timing and the harvest.

Ask for It and Work for It

Proverbs 16:26 says, "The appetite of laborers works for them; their hunger drives them on." How do you usually get something you really want? You ask for it, and then you work for it. When I was fifteen years old, I wanted a car. Since I knew my parents wouldn't buy it for me, I decided to buy it myself. To get what I wanted, I had to decide to work for it. I cut grass, hauled trash, and even spread black tar on driveways in 100-degree heat. My pursuit paid off when I paid for my 1979 black Camaro with cash. Hard work pays off, but it begins with a goal in mind and a plan to reach that goal. What goals are you pursuing currently?

> *Holy Spirit, move me toward action in*
> *pursuing and accomplishing the things*
> *that I tend to put off. Help me get after*
> *the tasks that are right in front of me.*

The Unmatched Value of Wisdom

How hard would you be willing to work in order to get something you really, really wanted? Proverbs 4:7 says, "The beginning of wisdom is this: Get wisdom. Though it cost all you have, get understanding." That's a rather strong statement to make. It assumes that wisdom is more valuable than pretty much anything we have. So what would you be willing to give up to acquire wisdom? Wisdom is more valuable than anything you currently have in your life, because without it, you can't make good choices that allow you to enjoy the rest of the life God has given you. So it makes sense that you'd work for wisdom over everything else.

Almighty God, I want to gain wisdom because of the value it has in my life as I follow you. I will give up other lesser pursuits to grab hold of the wisdom only you can give.

Actions, Not Intentions

What does your life say about what you actually believe in? It's easy to talk about convictions, character, patience, and love. But what does your work say about what's really embedded deeply in your heart? It's our actions, not our intentions, that reflect who we really are and what we truly believe. Proverbs 27:19 speaks to this simple truth: "As water reflects the face, so one's life reflects the heart." Take inventory of your daily habits. Look honestly at your schedule, at the activities and values you prioritize. And finally, look at your bank statements and your credit card bills. These will show you what's truly in your heart.

I want my heart to be your throne, Lord Jesus,
so show me the things that I need to rearrange
or remove in order for you to have first place.

Chasing Fantasies

Author Antoine de Saint-Exupéry said, "A goal without a plan is just a wish." This is one of the smartest, most practical things I've ever heard anyone say. If you have dreams for your future, they won't just magically happen. It's nice to fantasize about a better life, but until you make a plan and implement that plan with good old-fashioned hard work, it won't ever go anywhere. That's exactly what Proverbs 12:11 means when it says, "Those who work their land will have abundant food, but those who chase fantasies have no sense." Stop chasing fantasies. Order your life and prioritize your dream by rolling up your sleeves and getting to work.

> God, bless my efforts to put a plan in place
> to accomplish that task or goal I've been
> putting off. I won't wait any longer. It's
> time for me to get to work, and I will use
> this work as a way to worship you.

OTHERS

Know What to Avoid

For my wife and me, the busiest season of life occurred when our boys were little. Between school, ball practice, playdates, and doctor visits, it seemed like all we ever did was provide taxi service for our children. So we decided to redeem the time spent in the mini-van by memorizing Scripture with our boys. One verse we talked about regularly was Proverbs 22:5—"In the paths of the wicked are snares and pitfalls, but those who would preserve their life stay far from them." As adults, we can also benefit from applying this wisdom. Choose to avoid people, situations, and scenarios that might tempt you to compromise your convictions or sacrifice your integrity. Stay as far away from them as possible, no matter how harmless they may seem.

Holy Spirit, fill me with overflowing wisdom
so that I can steer clear of the traps and snares
the enemy would lay in front of me to stop
me from following your path for my life.

Keep Your Guard Up

When we get too busy, we often let our guard down. I've seen this deadly habit time and again in thirty-five years of ministry, especially in broken marriages. Late nights, sick kids, long hours, and heavy workloads can distract us from our primary relationships. I've counseled many couples on the verge of divorce because of an affair that slipped in through the cracks of a busy life. Proverbs 22:14 gives a stark warning of what happens when we succumb to that kind of temptation: "The mouth of an adulterous woman is a deep pit; a man who is under the LORD's wrath falls into it." Avoid the regret of a broken relationship by saying no to all the small things that would distract you from your one big yes—your marriage.

Lord, I ask for your protection over my heart, my marriage, and my family as I avoid any pitfall that the enemy may place in front of me.

The Company You Keep

confess that I've struggled with anger over the course of my life. I'm a passionate person, and I don't trend toward patience. Given these deep-seated tendencies, I've found it incredibly helpful to really meditate on Proverbs 22:24-25 as a warning and an encouragement. It says, "Do not make friends with a hot-tempered person, do not associate with one easily angered, or you may learn their ways and get yourself ensnared." In other words, be prudent about the company you keep—your comrades' habits will rub off on you. People with a short fuse and a hot head create trouble for themselves and those around them. So be careful to control your emotions, your frustration, and your reactions. Don't create a trap for yourself or a snare for the people around you.

*Reveal to me the deep places of impatience
and control that often cause me to lose my
temper, Lord, and give me patience to trust
you when I feel my blood begin to boil.*

Friends Who Are Friends of God

Who do you have in your life that you ask for advice? Can you name three people whose wisdom you seek before you make a big decision, whose counsel you request when you're struggling with something personally? We need godly friends we can trust, who we can call on when we can't see clearly or discern the way forward. The fact is, no matter how busy you are or what successes you've amassed, you must invest in friendships with people who are friends with God and his Word. Proverbs 24:6 says, "Surely you need guidance to wage war, and victory is won through many advisers." The best way to live a happy, fulfilled life is to fill it with the trusted voices of wise advisers who will steer you toward God—and away from the sinful temptations of this world.

Lord, help me find wise friends who will help me to grow in the fear and knowledge of you. Remind me to trust their voices and insight as I walk daily in your paths of righteousness.

Home as a Refuge

One way you can assess the health of your relationships is to monitor how you interact with the people closest to you, starting with your own family. If you begin to notice regular animosity or harsh words between you and your kids or your spouse, it could be a sign that you need to create time and space to reconnect with your loved ones emotionally. Few things are worse than living in a house where there's unspoken tension or unsettled conflict. Proverbs 25:24 says, "Better to live on the corner of the roof than share a house with a quarrelsome wife." Your home should be a place of peace and joy, an abode marked by safety and intimacy, not constant quarreling. Don't let anything create chaos or conflict in your house—deal with the issue, no matter what it takes.

Holy Spirit, make me sensitive to the
emotions and feelings of my family, and
help me notice any place where there is an
offense that I can work to reconcile.

Resolve to Reconcile

I s there anything more beautiful and life-giving than being at peace with the people you love? And is there anything more miserable than being at odds with someone you deeply care about? If you've ever had a big fight with your spouse or your boss or a good friend, you know that the resulting sense of unrest and disunity keeps you up at night until things are worked out. Is there an unresolved offense in a relationship with someone you love? That may be the soundtrack that's constantly playing in the background of your mind and emotions—a nonstop discordant hum that keeps you anxious and stressed out. Make a move. Take a first step today toward reconciliation with that person.

God, I am inspired to intentionally pursue reconciliation when I read Psalm 133:1 (ESV): "How good and pleasant it is when brothers dwell in unity."

Peace in Chaos

I n Matthew 5:39 Jesus tells us, "If anyone slaps you on the right cheek, turn to them the other cheek also." It's easy to forget that we represent the King of kings, who laid down his life as a sacrifice for sin. We're not called to vengefully repay those who hurt us. We get to do something more effective than that. We get to shine our light in this dark world. We get to practice kindness when others are attacking. We can remain calm when others are freaking out. We can smile while those around us shout. We can show the world that we have peace even when chaos abounds around us.

Jesus, there's no way I can forgive evil people in the power of my flesh or will. To live like you've commanded, I totally surrender to your power in me.

The Benefit of the Doubt

Ephesians 4:32 says, "Be kind and compassionate to one another, forgiving each other, just as in Christ God forgave you." Today, right now, call to mind this simple fact: Most people you come in contact with are not against God. They're probably doing their best to make it through another day, just like you. When you remind yourself that everyone is busy and has a lot on their plate, that most of us are running from one thing to the next, it's so much easier to give others the benefit of the doubt. It's also easier to pray for people when you remember that they're more like you than you probably realize. Treat others like Christ has treated you—with grace and patience.

I want to be more like you, Jesus. Help me speak with kindness and reach out to those around me with the same love and compassion that you've extended to me.

The Favor of God

Lots of preachers these days, it seems, are talking about God's favor. I've recently heard comments like "Favor ain't fair" and "I'm fighting for favor." Well, let me tell you that I have already found the favor of God in my life, and her name is Sharie King. She's my most trusted confidante, my chief advisor, my partner in ministry, and my wife. She's the best friend I've ever had, and I'd rather spend time with her than with anyone else on earth (no offense). Proverbs 18:22 says, "He who finds a wife finds what is good and receives favor from the LORD." Other than my salvation, Sharie is the best gift God ever gave me. Who has the Lord placed in your life as a sign of his favor and goodness? Take a minute and thank God for that person.

> *I know that the good people in my life who love me and bless me are all amazing gifts from you, heavenly Father. Thank you for caring for me through these people.*

You Can't Make Old Friends

heard a Kenny Rogers song on the radio called "You Can't Make Old Friends." I guess the point is you have to be a new friend first, and then years down the road, you can be considered an old friend. The Bible has much to say about the importance of friends. It also instructs us on the value of finding good friends, the kind of people who make you better, who challenge and inspire you, who love you enough to tell you the truth even if it hurts. Proverbs 27:17 says, "As iron sharpens iron, so one person sharpens another." This is the kind of friend we all need—a person who sharpens us and isn't afraid of the collision that's necessary for the sharpening to occur.

Lord, I want to be a better friend to the
people I love. Help me embody the character
and integrity needed to care for those
around me as you have cared for me.

Who Can Rebuke You?

I heard a sermon as a college student that quite literally changed my life. The pastor asked a question that stunned me: Who do you have in your life that can rebuke you when you're wrong and correct you when you make a mistake? At that moment, I realized I needed that person in my life—but I didn't really want that person in my life. Now, more than twenty years later, I have several people in my life who frequently point out things to me that I don't want to see or don't want to change, and these people are essential to my growth. Psalm 141:5 says, "Let a righteous man strike me—that is a kindness; let him rebuke me." Who do you have in your life that you've invited to speak truthfully to you? And if you have that person, do you listen to them? This kind of friend is a gift from God.

Lord, I want the blessings that come on
the other side of a wise and loving rebuke,
so bring people into my life who will
speak the truth even when it hurts.

Truly Trusted Friends

M ost of us had lots of friends when we were kids, because all that friendship required was being in the same class or playing at recess together. As we get older, we realize that truly trusted friends are few and far between. Sometimes I catch myself wondering who my real friends are, but then I'm reminded that I should also be asking myself how I can be a better friend to those around me. Proverbs 17:17 says, "A friend loves at all times, and a brother is born for a time of adversity." So instead of wondering which of my friends would stand with me in a time of hardship or suffering, I need to ask if I am the kind of man who stands by his friends when they're facing adversity in their lives. I want to be that kind of friend.

Jesus, I want to be a friend to others in the same way that you are a friend to me. Thank you for your example of staying faithful to your people, including me.

Growing Closer by Paying Attention

Proverbs 16:21 says, "The wise in heart are called discerning." I'm an extreme extrovert. I love people. They energize me. I've met tens of thousands of people in ministry over the past three decades, and I enjoy almost everyone I meet. It took me a while to discern, however, that not everyone in my family is like me, that if I don't pay attention to them, I can easily burn them out on church activities, dinners, outings, and events that people invite us to attend. God made each of us differently, as unique reflections of his image and character. Don't assume that those you love will love the things you love. Get to know your family members, their personalities, the things that give them life and the things that drain them of energy. It's one way we grow closer to those who are closest to us.

God, help me discern the differences in me and my family. Help me be sensitive to their feelings so that I can love them in a more tender and caring way.

Friends Who Hurt Your Feelings

Proverbs 17:10 says, "A rebuke impresses a discerning person more than a hundred lashes a fool." If you are wise, you will be impressed by someone who isn't worried about hurting your feelings but will tell you the truth in spite of how you may respond. A true friend isn't going to let you make a mistake without warning you of the possible consequences. You may think that your best friends would never hurt your feelings, but in reality the people who truly love you the most are willing to risk offending you to keep you from doing something foolish or harmful. Surround yourself with those kinds of friends, and become that kind of friend for others.

Lord, make me the kind of person who receives tough love from my friends. Form me into the kind of friend who's willing to give tough love when I need to.

The Mark of Christ in Your Life

As a pastor, I've preached a lot of funerals, and I know that people are not attracted to death—they come out of respect. People are drawn to life. Tens of thousands of fans will gather in stadiums to watch athletes compete or entertainers perform. Why? Because they're moving. They have life. When we work for the glory of God, people are drawn to him because of the life of Christ in us. Our daily conduct, the way we love people, the way we treat others—these are concrete steps we take to emulate Christ and reflect him to those around us, and they require hard work, but these very things also prove we've truly been saved and born again by believing the gospel of Jesus Christ. That's what Jesus meant when he said in John 13:35, "By this everyone will know that you are my disciples, if you love one another."

Jesus, I want to make the gospel attractive through how I live my life, so help me love people. Help me laugh and enjoy your gifts so that others see joy and life in me.

Coaching and Correction

Proverbs 15:31-32 says, "Whoever heeds life-giving correction will be at home among the wise. Those who disregard discipline despise themselves, but the one who heeds corrections gains understanding." I played sports all through college and had to get used to the idea that my coaches knew more than I did. As much as it pained me, I needed to listen to and obey them if I wanted to improve. Why would I resist the correction of a coach, someone wiser and more knowledgeable who sees what I don't see and understands what I don't know? That would be the definition of foolishness. Who do you listen to? Who do you trust to correct you, warn you, speak hard truth to you? You need those people in your life.

Holy Spirit, I want to be the kind of person who is humble enough to listen to wiser, smarter people. Develop that kind of humility in me.

Your Friendships and Your Future

My father used to say something all the time that still sticks with me to this day: "Show me a person's friendships, and I will show you their future." He knew that the people we hang out with will influence who we become, will affect the choices we make more than any other element or force in our lives. You can't pick your family, but you can pick your friends, so pick them according to their faith, their beliefs, their reputation, and their values. The future version of you will thank you one day for picking good friends and avoiding wicked, negative ones.

> *Lord, help me apply Proverbs 12:26 (NET)*
> *in my life as I choose my friendships: "The*
> *righteous person is cautious in his friendship,*
> *but the way of the wicked leads them astray."*

COMPARISONS

The Measure of Success

What motivates you to work hard? For many of us, it's the fear of not having enough, not being prepared for an emergency, or not measuring up to someone's expectations. For others, it may be a need to achieve success that results in the satisfaction of status or security. But Proverbs 22:4 offers a more helpful perspective on the way we should be measuring success and wealth: "Humility is the fear of the LORD; its wages are riches and honor and life." Maybe instead of working to grow the investment portfolio or to provide more opportunities for our kids, we should be measuring our riches in how humble we are in relation to God and his grace, mercy, and goodness. That's a much better metric to gauge our success.

God, I praise you for the wealth and riches you have freely given me through the life, death, and resurrection of Jesus Christ, my Savior.

Glory Is Primary

Comparison comes in many forms. We can envy someone's family, job, or income. We can be jealous of another person's body, their looks, their weight, or even their education. This isn't just something teenagers struggle with. Comparison follows us into adulthood and can feel hard to overcome. Much of the stress that causes Americans so much anxiety results from the feeling that we don't measure up to the successes and achievements of others. Proverbs 23:17 encourages us, "Do not let your heart envy sinners, but always be zealous for the fear of the LORD." When we care more about pleasing God than we do about measuring up to self-imposed expectations, envy will diminish, and God's glory becomes our primary goal.

*Lord, I admit that I envy others at times. I repent
of the sin of comparison and confess that because
you love me, I have no cause for jealousy in my life.*

Seeing the Full Picture

If you ever find yourself feeling frustrated when you see ungodly people prospering, remember that what you see in front of you is only a snapshot and not the full picture. Don't waste time worrying why people who cut corners, lie, or walk all over others seem to be doing better than you. In the end, it will all amount to nothing, so continue to commit your life and work to Christ, live with integrity, and don't stress over what seems like the successes of wicked people. God sees everything, and God has the last word. Proverbs 24:19-20 is a promise that can bring peace when you feel discouraged at the success of the wicked: "Do not fret because of evildoers or be envious of the wicked, for the evildoer has no future hope, and the lamp of the wicked will be snuffed out."

Jesus, give me a more eternal perspective so that I can see what you see and value what you value, trusting the eventual outcomes to your wisdom and sound judgment.

Managing Your Own Business

In our interconnected world of Facebook and Instagram and Twitter, we're all spending more time reading what other people say and looking at what other people post: pictures of food and kids and vacations, political and social opinions, and the obligatory cat video. But is it a good use of your time to scroll through social media feeds just to get sucked into the drama of people that you don't even live with? Proverbs 26:17 speaks to this: "Like one who grabs a stray dog by the ears is someone who rushes into a quarrel not their own." You are not obligated to comment, or to even care, about the opinions of other people. You can choose to avoid it. Walk away. Keep your mouth closed. And as soon as you can, get back to managing your own life.

Jesus, help me not be pulled away from my responsibilities by the opinions, the voices, or the drama of others. I have enough to do without getting involved elsewhere.

The Craving for Affirmation

In our current age of instant response and engagement, one post or one tweet can get immediate "likes" or "follows," and that can feed our ego, making us think we're way bigger and better than we really are. Our egos are fragile, and when not submitted to the lordship of Christ, we can crave constant affirmation from others to make us feel important. But this is a dead-end road. We are already loved by God. Jesus has already died in our place and been raised from the dead for our salvation. Instead of waiting on others to celebrate you, rest in God's love for you. Remember Proverbs 27:21, which says, "The crucible for silver and the furnace for gold, but people are tested by their praise."

I admit that I love being noticed sometimes,
God. But ultimately, it's only your approval
and acceptance that matter to me.

Initiate Kindness

I believe that Christians should be the friendliest people on earth. We have the joy of our salvation and the presence of the Holy Spirit with us every day, and others should see that in us. When Sharie and I got married, she was surprised that I waved at every car I passed while driving. She'd always ask me if I knew the drivers, and I would say no, that I was just being friendly. I grew up in a small town where this was common, but she was from Atlanta, where no one ever waved at a stranger! There was definitely a shift in perspective for both of us—and this can be a reminder that sometimes a simple act of kindness makes all the difference. Colossians 3:12 says, "As God's chosen people… clothe yourselves with compassion, kindness." Instead of comparing yourself with others, initiate kindness, and your love will reflect the love of Christ.

*Holy Spirit, will you inspire me today to
reach out to someone—with no intention
or agenda except to lift them up and
encourage them with a kind word?*

Don't Wait, Initiate

When Jesus taught the Scriptures and talked about the kingdom of God, he loved to challenge the way people usually thought about life. For instance, in Matthew 5:47 he asked his audience hard questions: "If you greet only your own people, what are you doing more than others? Do not even pagans do that?" In other words, the people of God are compelled by the love of God to actually love the kinds of people who may not love them back. As Christians, we don't compare our love with the world's love. We practice a kind of love that takes the first step—we don't wait on the other person to do something for us. We show others what God is like by extending grace and kindness regardless of how they treat us. This is how the love of God becomes a reality in our lives.

Jesus, I don't want to wait on others to love me first. I want to initiate kindness and grace with others so they will see your love flowing in me and through me.

Progress, Not Perfection

Personal transformation is proven by our actions. James 3:13-14 (csb) says, "Who among you is wise and understanding? By his good conduct he should show that his works are done in the gentleness that comes from wisdom. But if you have bitter envy and selfish ambition in your heart, don't boast and deny the truth." You know you're growing in wisdom by the way you live. Transformation means changing your ways by God's grace and power, not by comparing your spiritual progress to others. You do this simply by acting in ways that glorify God, drawing attention to him and his work in our hearts through the Holy Spirit.

I want to grow in wisdom, Holy Spirit. I want to increase in understanding. Fill me with your power and give me insight into matters that I could not know without your guidance.

The Right Thing for the Right Reason

Proverbs 21:2 (CSB) says, "All a person's ways seem right to him, but the LORD weighs hearts." God knows why we do the things we do and whether we do them for the right reasons or the wrong ones. It's good to do the right thing, but it's even better to do the right thing for the right reason. We can't always tell the true motivation behind our good actions, and we often find ourselves doing something good so we will look good compared to others—or so others will see us and be impressed. We all want to put our best foot forward. Yet we often make mistakes because we make decisions based on how we can get something that we want rather than considering what is best for someone else.

Remind me today, heavenly Father, that you see what I do but you also see why I do it. Help my motivations to be pure and holy, with a desire to please you most of all.

Look at What You're Looking At

One of the original Ten Commandments was the charge not to covet. It simply means a desire, born of jealousy or greed, to possess what other people have. Be careful what you gaze upon, because there are countless ways now to view the possessions and successes of others. Proverbs 27:20 warns, "Death and Destruction are never satisfied, and neither are human eyes." If you find yourself giving in to insecurity or comparison, the simplest way to fight back is to avert your eyes. Look away. Turn off the device. Delete the app. Get off social media for a while. You alone control where your eyes look. Take authority over them and point them away from temptation.

Help me guard my eyes, Holy Spirit, by turning them away from the things of this world that promise me pleasure but fail when compared with your eternal worth.

Nothing to Prove

One practical way you can defeat comparison and insecurity is to ask yourself why you take it to heart when you feel overlooked. The reason it stings so badly could possibly reveal the source of your insecurity. People completely grounded in the love of Jesus are less likely to get bent out of shape when someone says something hurtful to them. When you know you have nothing to prove, when you allow what God thinks about you to define your self-image, then you are not worried about what other people think about you. You are given validation and worth by the amazing truth that you are God's son or daughter. You don't need to do anything else.

> *Because my identity is rooted in you and*
> *not what others think about me, Lord,*
> *I can celebrate the truth of Proverbs 10:9—*
> *"Whoever walks in integrity walks securely."*

DISTRACTIONS

Live Your Own Life

When people say things like "I'm just so busy—I don't have time to exercise or eat right or go to church," I often ask them how much time they spend scrolling social media on their phone. And your phone will tell you with accuracy just how many moments of your day you waste watching other people live their lives when you could be living yours. Galatians 5:15 speaks to the danger of entertaining the drama or the facades that other people create. It says plainly, "If you bite and devour each other, watch out or you will be destroyed by each other." Decide that you have better ways to spend your time than watching people say ugly, negative, untrue things about others. Avoiding this kind of false witness will prolong your life and increase your joy as well as your effectiveness.

Father, help me ignore the distractions and drama that surround me so that I can tune my ear to your loving, faithful voice of grace.

No Need to Know It All

t's hard for driven, success-oriented people like me to let things go, especially when we need to understand why something is the way it is (or when we need to be right). I wonder how much time I've wasted over the years reading long articles, clicking on links to opinion pieces on issues that really don't matter to me or my family or my faith in the long run. Do you have an unhealthy need to always understand everything? That may be hurting you in the long run. Proverbs 25:27 says, "It is not good to eat too much honey, nor is it honorable to search out matters that are too deep." Don't waste precious time searching out matters that have no impact on your life—use that time to invest in nurturing close relationships with your family and friends.

God, by your grace I will accept that there are certain things I will never know and millions of things I don't need to understand. I know you love me, and that's enough.

Stop Wasting Time and Energy

In the age of social media, we're given access to an endless flood of other people's opinions and ideas. And countless numbers of total strangers also have access to us through what we share and post. I've learned a small but powerful lesson: Never engage online with someone who only wants to fight or argue, especially if you don't know the person. Trust me, you can never win. And why would you want to? It's not your job to correct or sway or make a point with someone you've never even met. Proverbs 26:4 warns, "Do not answer a fool according to his folly, or you yourself will be just like him." You don't owe strangers access to you or your time. Instead, choose consciously to pour your time and energy into the people you know and love and can have a face-to-face conversation with.

God, I choose to spend my time investing
in the people who matter most to me, and
I will not waste my time or energy on
foolish fights or silly arguments.

The Pursuit of Peace

You probably don't think of yourself as a trouble-maker. No one does. I've never met someone who upon introduction said, "I stir up drama and cause stress for other people." But as a Christian, you shouldn't be satisfied with simply not creating drama. You should prioritize avoiding stressful situations when possible and working for peace. That's what Proverbs 26:21 means when it says, "As charcoal to embers and as wood to fire, so is a quarrelsome person for kindling strife." In the same way that fire can simmer and then erupt to destroy a home, a divisive person can ignite conflict that hurts everyone involved. Decide that you will not be that kind of person, but instead will work for peace and reconciliation in relationships with others.

Heavenly Father, I want to be a person of peace. Show me ways I can work to build bridges of love and hope with others, not create boundaries between them.

Understanding over Opinions

I t seems like our culture right now is one big shouting match where everyone has an opinion and they want everyone else to know about it. News outlets and social media have given us all a platform to share what we think about everything from politics to preachers. But this is not necessarily a good thing, and as a matter of fact, vocalizing our own opinions excessively can leave us looking foolish. Consider the words of Proverbs 18:2—"Fools find no pleasure in understanding but delight in airing their own opinions." So the wisdom of God's Word would direct us to spend less time distracted by countless opinions and more time seeking understanding.

Remind me today, Father, that you have given me two ears and just one mouth so that I will listen twice as much as I speak.

You Don't Have to Listen

've learned a valuable lesson in life and ministry. Do not trust a person who comes to you and gossips about someone else. If they slander a person behind their back to you, then you can bet that they would likely slander you behind your back to someone else eventually. Gossiping is a character issue and a bad habit, and it is also addictive. Proverbs 20:19 says, "A gossip betrays a confidence; so avoid anyone who talks too much." In order to keep the poison of gossip out of your system, decide that you will not be distracted by hearsay. Avoid it. With kindness and clarity, you have the power to say, "I would rather not hear you speak poorly of them to me. It's not right, and I don't want to listen."

Going forward, Lord, I will avoid the kind of people that spread rumors and speak negatively about others. Forgive me when I've done this myself.

Goodwill Toward Others

I n the hustle and bustle of your daily life, distractions are the norm. The phone is always giving you a notification, the texts keep coming, and the email inbox keeps piling up. But one small thing that you can do to bring harmony and peace into the push and pull of your life is simply this: Be a friendly person. It's an easy way to avoid conflict. Proverbs 18:1 says, "An unfriendly person pursues selfish ends and against all sound judgment starts quarrels." A friendly disposition puts others at ease and defuses difficult situations before they get out of control. A smile, a pat on the shoulder, a kind word—these simple gestures of goodwill and charity go a long way in a busy world where one word can blow up into a big misunderstanding.

Jesus, I don't ever want to be the kind of person that starts a quarrel, so I ask for your grace to restrain me when I am tempted to vent my anger or frustration.

Not Addicted to Drama

Have you noticed how media outlets love to blow a situation out of proportion just to get your attention? Sensationalized headlines clamor for our attention in hopes of using bad news or drama to capture us for just a moment, usually long enough to try to sell us something. It's called clickbait nowadays, but it's just a new version of the same old thing: We sometimes find ourselves distracted by someone else's crisis. Proverbs 17:19 says, "Whoever loves a quarrel loves sin." Isn't that interesting? When we devote time and energy to fighting, drama, gossip, or someone else's quarrel, the end result is always sinful. What's worse, we grow to love it. Don't become addicted to drama—walk away before you get sucked in.

Jesus, I will fill my mind with your holy Word and replace any negative appetite for drama and fighting with the wisdom of the Bible.

When Hurting Helps

I recently had my appendix removed, and it was one of the worst and most painful experiences of my life. After my appendix burst, I developed sepsis, and I needed months to get my strength and appetite back. I became close with my surgeon and realized that the scars on my body were a result of his careful attempts to save my life. But he had to wound me, to cut into my body, in order to remove the problem. Proverbs 27:6 says, "Wounds from a friend can be trusted, but an enemy multiplies kisses." Understand that God loves you enough to offend you and convict you when you're wrong, but he's not trying to hurt you. He's trying to help you. Don't be distracted by the pain. Welcome the wounds! They're for your good.

Father, I appreciate your willingness to hurt me in ways that actually help me. I will embrace the pain for my own good and growth.

Saying No to Negativity

One small but powerful discipline that helps you grow spiritually is the awareness of your own emotions, particularly when they creep up on you. Proverbs 27:4 mentions three negative feelings: "Anger is cruel and fury overwhelming, but who can stand before jealousy?" Negative emotions sap you of your strength. They make you weak, to the point that you can't stand, or endure, their effects. When you sense discouragement or sadness, don't let the way you're feeling distract you. Instead, name the feeling. Say it out loud. Hiding your jealousy or anger can lead to shame, so disarm those difficult feelings by exposing them to the light. Confess the feelings to God and ask the Holy Spirit to help you. You'll be surprised how quickly he will answer you.

Today, Jesus, I will not let my feelings rule me. I will acknowledge my emotions, but I will also submit them to you as my Lord and King.

Discernment amid the Distractions

It's becoming more difficult to know what to believe these days because there are so many sources of information and so many distractions on our screens. How can we know who, and what, to trust? Don't believe everything you hear. You have an advantage because you have the Holy Spirit living in you and he can guide you internally to discern what is right and what is wrong, what is true and what is false. Have you asked the Spirit to help you? Do you daily invite him to show you what to believe and what to reject? It's his job to do so, and his joy to help us.

Holy Spirit, I ask you today to help me know the truth as I remember Proverbs 14:15, which says, "The simple believe anything, but the prudent give thought to their steps."

BLESSED

Maximize Your Message

At the beginning of the Sermon on the Mount, Matthew 5:1 notes that when Jesus saw the crowds, he went up on a mountainside, and after he sat down, he began to teach. I've been to the place where this happened according to tradition, and it's compelling to see the spot where Jesus preached his most famous sermon. He picked a location where people could hear him; he used the backdrop of a steep hill and the amplifying power of the water in front of him to maximize his message. This is how Jewish rabbis often taught their disciples. Today, Jesus is still trying to get his gospel to as many people as possible, and the way he maximizes his message is through his followers, his disciples, as we live out the message of the gospel to the world around us.

Lord, I want to use my voice to share your gospel with the world. Magnify my words, not for my glory but for the good of others and the growth of your kingdom.

Holiness from Hard Things

I grew up hearing my pastor talk about the *Beatitudes*—and that word always sounded weird to me as a kid. But when I learned what they were and where they came from, I realized how important they are in the lives of people following Jesus. In Matthew 5, Jesus points out people who are most blessed, using the word *blessed* nine different times in eight verses. These are the Beatitudes, the blessings that God promises to his children. It comes from the ancient Latin word meaning "happy," but the interesting thing about these blessings is how Jesus connects them with hard times and suffering. It's a new way to look at life; sometimes happiness and blessing lie on the other side of something really difficult that God will use to prove his faithfulness.

> *Jesus, I submit my seasons of suffering into your nail-scarred hands. I want the hard things I go through to forge holiness inside my heart. May your will be done.*

A Deeper Joy

In Matthew 5:3 Jesus says, "Blessed are the poor in spirit, for theirs is the kingdom of heaven." Doesn't it strike you as odd that Jesus would connect blessing with a kind of poverty? But this is not a poverty of money or possessions. Being poor in spirit can mean discouragement, disappointment, or even depression. Let this encourage you today, that even when you are at your lowest point emotionally or spiritually, you can find a deeper joy rooted in Jesus and his heavenly kingdom. The blessing of knowing Jesus and the promise of his kingdom are better than the momentary happiness that's dependent on your current circumstances. Stay focused on the kingdom of heaven, and it will help you get through the hard times you face here on earth.

> *Today, God, I will turn my eyes away from the difficult things that surround me, and I will cast my gaze toward heaven, where you have prepared a place for me for eternity.*

The Comfort of the Holy Spirit

Of all the hard things I've ever had to do, nothing comes close to preaching my father's funeral—on Father's Day. He was a great man of God, and I was honored to have the last word before we buried his body. It took me several years to grieve his death. The mourning process for me was unpredictable and difficult, but over and over again I remembered the words of Jesus from Matthew 5:4—"Blessed are those who mourn, for they will be comforted." There is a kind of comfort the Holy Spirit gives a person when they're mourning the death of a loved one, a consolation and solace that we can only experience in a time of great loss. So lean into this promise from Jesus that his comfort will be there for you when you need it most.

Reveal to me, Holy Spirit, any painful portion of my heart that I have not yet fully allowed you to heal. Fill the wounded places with your peace and comfort.

The Power of Humility

When I think about famous people who have ruled the earth, certain names come to mind: Julius Caesar, Genghis Khan, Alexander the Great, the pharaohs and Roman emperors and military conquerors. And what words describe these famous rulers? *Strength. Ambition. Conquest. Aggression.* There is one word, however, that never comes to mind when I think about these acclaimed rulers: *humility.* Would you believe, though, that Jesus actually says that the humble will one day inherit the earth? He makes that promise in Matthew 5:5—"Blessed are the meek." But notice one small, key difference. Earthly rulers must conquer in order to gain anything of value. The children of God will rule the earth not by conquering it but by inheriting it from their heavenly Father. Jesus already conquered sin and death, and it humbles us to know that he did it for us! We will inherit the earth that he died to redeem.

Oh Jesus, what a great victory you won for me on the cross! The earth is yours, and I am too. Thank you for the spiritual inheritance you've given me.

God Is the Greatest Blessing

I pretty much stay hungry all the time. I like to tell people that one of my spiritual gifts is eating. Like most of us, I was blessed to have access to food growing up, and now, as an adult, I never wonder where my next meal is coming from. But the people of Galilee whom Jesus taught in Matthew 5 were different—they lived from day to day, from season to season, never knowing if the rain would fall or if the crops would grow. They knew what it was like to be truly hungry and thirsty. So when Jesus promises in Matthew 5:6 that those who hunger and thirst for righteousness will be filled and blessed, they picked up on that promise. It's a good thing in the kingdom of God to be hungry, to crave more of God's presence, more of his grace, more of his peace in your life. We are happiest when we're pursuing God and not just the things that God gives us.

Almighty God, if you never gave me another blessing or another gift, I could never praise you enough for how much you have already provided for me in this life. Thank you!

Forgive, Forget, Repeat

It seems like it's human nature for us to want to get even with people when they hurt us. As a kid on the playground, I remember telling my friends I was going to "get back at" a boy who pushed me off the monkey bars at recess, and I did when I pushed him off a swing. But that kind of retribution at any age of life never accomplishes anything good. We may feel good for a moment, but it never lasts. In Matthew 5:7 Jesus speaks to this when he says, "Blessed are the merciful, for they will be shown mercy." And this makes sense, right? When you show mercy to others, they will return mercy back to you when you need it. The alternative is tragic—a world where everyone is trying to get even and settle scores and no one shows mercy to anyone.

If you want to be happy, then forgive, forget, and extend the kind of mercy to others that Jesus extended to you.

Jesus, because you showed me great mercy when you died in my place on the cross, I am able today to extend the same kind of undeserved mercy to anyone who crosses or offends me.

Clean Hearts and Pure Motives

When my wife and I traveled to Italy for our twentieth anniversary, we visited dozens of old churches and monasteries and saw hundreds of paintings and pictures of Jesus. Ironically, he looked very European in most of those paintings. It's normal to want to see God, and you don't need special glasses or spiritual 4D goggles. You just need a pure heart that craves a glimpse of your heavenly Father. Jesus promised us in Matthew 5:8, "Blessed are the pure in heart, for they will see God." We can see the work of God and the presence of his Spirit all around us when we keep our hearts clean and our motives pure by looking for God instead of always looking for other things to ultimately satisfy us.

I know that you alone, Lord, can truly satisfy me. Help me remove the blinders from my eyes so I can see just how beautiful and breathtaking your glory really is.

Ambassadors of Peace

As parents, Sharie and I spent a decade trying to negotiate peace between our two sons. They hit and kicked and pinched and bit each other; they body-slammed each other and jumped off of objects onto one another. Eventually, they made peace, and now they are the best of friends. The process of being a peacemaker is often taxing and frustrating, but the end result is worth all the effort, because the end product is people living at peace with each other. And isn't that what we all want? Jesus understood this when he promised in Matthew 5:9, "Blessed are the peacemakers, for they will be called children of God." Nothing you can do with your life will bless others more abundantly, and make you happier, than bringing peace into the lives of those around you. It brings God glory, and it brings us joy and blessing.

> *God, I want to be a peacemaker. It's in my spiritual DNA, and I want to access your power to bring peace with me everywhere I go as your ambassador in this world.*

Do the Right Thing

Doing the right thing is always right, but we can't always expect to be applauded or celebrated when we do what's right in God's eyes. Actually, standing for what is good and righteous and holy will sometimes be quite unpopular. Even if it means we're persecuted or ridiculed, we can hold fast to the promise Jesus made in Matthew 5:10 when he said, "Blessed are those who are persecuted because of righteousness, for theirs is the kingdom of heaven." So remember that a little bit of ridicule for your faith now is nothing compared to what you have to look forward to in eternity: forever with Jesus in the new heaven and the new earth, in a new kingdom that will last forever.

Jesus, you are worth more than the applause of the world. Your glory is more valuable than being noticed and rewarded by anyone on this earth. I live for your approval.

An Eternal Perspective

Our culture seems to assume that bad things shouldn't happen to good people. The thinking goes like this: If you live a good life and don't do anything too bad, if you're kind to animals and recycle, if you reduce your carbon footprint and obey the speed limit, and if you're nice to people in general, then life should go well for you. But while those are all good things, just doing good things does not guarantee any of us an easy life. As 1 John 2:17 says, "The world and its desires pass away, but whoever does the will of God lives forever." The hard things we go through here will pale in comparison to the joy we'll know spending forever in the new heaven and the new earth with Jesus. Let's keep an eternal perspective and not assume that we deserve an easy life here. Our best life is yet to come.

Remind me today, Lord, that the greatest pleasures I've ever experienced here in this life are nothing compared to what waits for me in the new heaven and the new earth.

Turning Adversaries into Allies

I n Matthew 5:44-45 Jesus includes these words in his Sermon on the Mount: "I tell you, love your enemies and pray for those who persecute you, that you may be children of your Father in heaven." What a massive paradigm shift—Christ's listeners had literally never heard anything like this before. You were supposed to hate your enemies and fight those who came against you. The goal was to defeat your enemies—in their case, the Roman Empire. But Jesus is announcing a new way of thinking, a new way of living. He is building a new kingdom where our enemies become our friends, our adversaries become our allies, and we show the world how good and beautiful the Lord is by how we love others.

Loving Father, I am your child and your representative here on this earth. My desire is to show the world what you look like, who you are, and how you love.

Question Your Assumptions

If you've ever questioned why God would let bad things happen to you, that line of thought is usually based on the assumption that you think you're a pretty good person, that it just makes sense that good things should happen to you. I've wondered the same thing, and it can be frustrating, especially when we see seemingly good things happening to people who do bad things. It turns out that we're not the first to wonder about this. Jesus spoke to this question in Matthew 5:45 when he said that God "causes his sun to rise on the evil and the good, and sends rain on the righteous and the unrighteous." The Lord wants us to understand that he doesn't reward us and punish us in this life according to our assumptions. God's blessings fall on the saved and the sinner because he loves us all.

I confess to you, God, that I cannot understand the deep mysteries of your plans. But what I cannot know, I will accept by faith, entrusting the results to you.

Love Without Conditions

'm sure you've heard the saying "You scratch my back and I'll scratch yours." You do something good for someone, and they return the favor. While there's nothing wrong with this perspective, Jesus takes it a step further and challenges his followers to think differently. In Matthew 5:46 he says, "If you love those who love you, what reward will you get? Are not even the tax collectors doing that?" At that time it was common practice for tax collectors to cheat the Jewish people by taking more money from them than they should, often calling in favors from people in their debt. But Jesus wants us to go beyond that practice: He wants us to love people who can't do anything for us. In doing so, he will bless us.

Father, help me love people who are hard
to love and forgive people who are hard to
forgive, bearing in mind that I, too, am
often hard to love and hard to forgive.

Anonymous Generosity

I n Matthew 6:2 Jesus said, "When you give to the needy, do not announce it with trumpets, as the hypocrites do in the synagogues and on the streets, to be honored by others. Truly I tell you, they have received their reward in full." He's pointing out the common practice of religious leaders who didn't really care about helping the poor—they only cared about being seen by the crowds and being honored for their charity. Let's make sure we don't become like the Pharisees. And the best way to avoid that temptation is to practice anonymous generosity as often as possible. Do something good for someone without anyone knowing about it. You will both be blessed, and you'll be rewarded by our heavenly Father.

Purify my motives, heavenly Father, and remind me that you see everything I do, but more importantly, you also see the real reason I do it.

Eternal Reward

As I read the Gospels, I'm fascinated by how often Jesus talks about God rewarding those who follow him. In Matthew 6:3-4 Jesus says, "When you give to the needy, do not let your left hand know what your right hand is doing, so that your giving may be in secret. Then your Father, who sees what is done in secret, will reward you." This tells us that it's not wrong for us to expect God to bless our obedience and our faithfulness. The ultimate reward is Jesus, but Jesus himself promises that when we do God's will, and we do it God's way, the Lord himself will see that obedience. But will he ignore it? No, on the contrary, he will reward it. So be encouraged: God sees you. Your Father, who loves you and cares for you so deeply, is watching you live your life for his glory and has planned for you a reward beyond your wildest dreams.

God, I want to do your will, and I want to do it your way. Give me the ability to submit my will to yours, trusting that you will reward my obedience.

Refined Through the Fire

Most parents want to provide a good life for their children, a life better than the one they had when they were kids, but sometimes this can backfire—and not just for parents. It's not always a good thing when everything is easy for us. Proverbs 29:21 says, "A servant pampered from youth will turn out to be insolent." We often refer to people like this as spoiled, and it happens when the path is easy and we never face adversity. But thankfully God doesn't spoil us. He blesses us, and he uses the hard things we go through to form our integrity and refine our values, to build our resilience and cultivate our character. Hardship helps us learn to rely on him alone for provision.

*Heavenly Father, I don't want to pray
away the hard things in life. I want to
see them as opportunities to grow deeper
in my dependence on you instead of as
things I need to automatically avoid.*

Prepared for Eternity

It's not healthy to dwell on death, but it's imperative that you consider the inevitability of your eventual demise and make sure you have a plan for your eternity. That's why a Christian doesn't have to fear the end of their earthly life. We know that heaven awaits us, that Jesus has prepared a place for us. When we live with our eternal home in view, we work differently, we worry less, we hold things with open hands because we know our treasure is in heaven. The sad fate for unbelievers is starkly different. Proverbs 11:7 (CSB) says, "When a wicked person dies, his expectation comes to nothing, and hope placed in wealth vanishes."

Jesus, thank you that because of your resurrection from the dead, I can have certainty that my life will not perish when I die but will continue on forever with you in heaven.

Who You Really Are

In all aspects of your life, seek to honor the Lord in how you live. The way you treat your kids, the way you pay your taxes, the attitude you have toward people of different ethnicities and backgrounds—all these things reflect who you really are. You can't hide what's truly in your heart, and your life will reveal what really matters most to you. God already knows what you truly believe, and one day it will all be revealed. If your ways are blameless, you have nothing to worry about because God blesses and takes joy in the person who lives consistently with honor.

God, today my prayer is that I will be the kind of person you delight in from Proverbs 11:20—"The LORD detests those whose hearts are perverse, but he delights in those whose ways are blameless."

One-Minute Prayers® for Women
Hope Lyda

One-Minute Prayers® for Men
Harvest House Publishers

One-Minute Prayers® to Unwind a Worried Mind
Hope Lyda

One-Minute Prayers® to Start Your Day
Hope Lyda

One-Minute Prayers® for Young Women
Hope Lyda

One-Minute Prayers® for Young Men
Clayton King

One-Minute Prayers® for Leaders
Steve Miller

CROSSROADS
SUMMER CAMP

THE BEST WEEK
OF YOUR SUMMER!

CAMP PASTOR
CLAYTON KING

CROSSROADSSUMMERCAMP.COM

CKM
SPEAKERS
LOOKING FOR A SPEAKER FOR YOUR NEXT EVENT?
BOOK A CKM SPEAKER TODAY!
CLAYTONKING.COM/SPEAKERS